P9-AQA-306

Course in Effective Thinking

Hugh P. O'Neill, S.J.

LOYOLA UNIVERSITY PRESS
Chicago 60657

Produced in book form April 1964.

INTRODUCTION

This Course in Effective Thinking was first offered to freshmen at the University of Detroit on a non-credit basis in 1939. It was devised by Reverend Hugh P. O'Neill, S.J. in an attempt to help students acquire proper study habits upon which success in college largely depends. The series of drills or problems were therefore aimed at challenging the student's powers of observation, analysis, invention, and classification. Small groups (no more than ten in a group) met twice a week for eight weeks. At times the enrollment reached as high as two hundred, divided into twenty groups. Almost from the beginning the course was staffed by highly competent junior and senior students who were preparing for a teaching career.

In later years many of the young men and women who had tutored the course reported that this experience paid rich dividends when they first found themselves facing high-school classes. Many University of Detroit students who entered the armed services and were required to take qualifying tests as part of their induction routine felt very much at home with these tests by reason of their similarity to the drills they had taken at the University. A number of applicants for graduate school attributed their success in analogy tests, administered at entrance, to the training they had received in the Course in Effective Thinking.

Over the years the course has been used in a considerable number of seminaries, in novitiates of religious orders, and in an adult-education group. Individual teachers have made use of it in various high schools as well as in state and private colleges and universities.

Testimonies from many sources to the value of the course and continued requests for copies of the course materials have persuaded the author to have his work published in book form.

Those who are concerned about the deficiencies of college students not only in ability to use basic thought processes but in intellectual curiosity, right emotional attitudes, desirable personality traits and even adequate vocabulary and self-expression, will discover that this Course in Effective Thinking is far from just another how to study manual. It is instead a practical and powerful invitation to learning. It is both remedial and constructive. It teaches the student how to learn by actually challenging him in drill and discussion to acquire one after another the numerous all-important elements which together constitute the substance of effective study habits.

The tutor or teacher who adopts this course will find that the author's topics for discussion connected with each of the drills and his analysis of typical student defects and their remedies will make the task of conducting the course lighter for himself and more profitable for the student. He will be surprised how much he will learn about human nature!

While the course is primarily intended for use with college freshmen or high-school seniors, the materials will be found admirably suited to the needs of more mature persons who are planning to resume a program of study after a more or less prolonged interruption.

Allan P. Farrell, S.J.

January 10, 1964
University of Detroit

CONTENTS

Purpose

The Course in Effective Thinking comprises a set of materials and a technique to be used in tutoring pupils in the fundamental thought processes which are essential in the formation of good study habits. The program may be described as a course in informal logic.

In addition to positive training in thinking, the course envisages the following secondary but very important results.

1 It enables the tutor to secure an intimate acquaintance with the abilities and the mental habits of the individual pupil. This opens the way to the discovery and correction of defects, most of which will be found to be rooted in wrong emotional attitudes and undesirable personality traits, such as heedlessness, stubbornness, superficiality, and diffidence.

2 It brings home to the pupil the fact that he has been going through life with his eyes half closed to the world in which he is living, that he is woefully ignorant of many basic facts of everyday life, and that he has seldom done any real thinking about the most familiar objects and ideas. It also makes him conscious of the inadequacy of his vocabulary.

3 It enables the tutor to stimulate intellectual curiosity by introducing discussions of interesting bits of information in the fields of literature, science, government, commerce, and industry. These discussions, of course, will have real value only if conducted in such a way as to lead the pupil to seek further information and understanding on his own initiative.

4 The spirited discussions, which are the normal outcome of the proper use of the drills, will give the pupil frequent opportunity for the exercise of self-expression, and the facility thus gained will carry over into his work in other classes, his public speaking, and his general conversation.

Subject Matter

The material used in the course consists of several series of drills which challenge the pupil's powers of observation, analysis, invention, classification, and so forth. The problems consist of word groups which are to be analyzed, classified, revised, and completed. These problems resemble the materials used in standard intelligence tests, but the use that is made of them is entirely different from the technique of intelligence testing. The primary purpose of this course is to train minds, not to test them, and the diagnostic value of the work results not from the inspection of objective scores, but from the personal observation of the tutor.

Procedure

The tutor presents his pupils with a set of problems, either by writing them on the blackboard or by issuing mimeographed sheets. A maximum of fifteen minutes is allowed for the solution of these problems and the recording of answers. At the end of this writing period, the tutor calls upon his pupils individually for an oral report on their solutions. As each answer is given, it is discussed by the group under the direction of the tutor. Alternate answers are proposed and compared with one another. Sometimes two or three answers are found to be valid. When this happens, an effort is made to determine which is most significant, most scientific, and so forth.

After the most suitable answer is agreed upon, the tutor will do well to make sure that the pupils have a clear understanding of the exact meaning of each word that occurs in the problem. He may also take occasion to bring out some point of science, history, government, or literature that may be suggested by the subject matter of the problem. The choice of topics and the trend of the discussion will depend chiefly on the cultural background and the pedagogical instincts of the tutor. He should avoid spending too much time on any given topic. During the discussion the tutor should be on the alert to notice defective attitudes manifested by individual pupils. He should use his own judgment in deciding whether these defects should be corrected in class or in private conference.

It is our experience that this type of work can be done only with small groups. The number of pupils in any one group should never exceed ten, and best results will be achieved if only seven are taken at one time. It is suggested that the course be given for six or eight weeks, with three class periods a week. For the sake of variety the tutor will do well to take different types of drills on successive class days. It has been found desirable to have pupils assign grades to their performance in the written part of the test and to keep a record of these grades.

Nature of Thought Processes

The Course in Effective Thinking is inspired by the following description of elementary thought processes. All thinking is either comparative or inventive. Comparison consists in seeking differences or similarities between two or more words, objects, or ideas, or between parts of the same object or idea. The search for differences is characteristic of analysis, the search for similarities leads to synthesis. Classification is a combination of both, for in classification we put similar things together and keep dissimilar things apart. Invention consists in looking for a new element, a word, an object, or an idea, which will supplement a given situation. Thus we must find or make a key to fit a given lock, we must seek a suitable site before we can proceed to put up a given type of building. A doctor must find suitable remedies for given diseases, a mechanic must build a certain type of machine to perform a predetermined operation. In invention we first analyze what we have and determine precisely what we need, and then go out and make or find the new element which is needed to complete the synthesis.

In administering the drills, the tutor should take frequent occasion to explain to his pupils the particular type of thinking that they are asked to perform, and should try to make it clear to them that the most philosophic and scientific thought consists in nothing else than the refined and automatic use of these simple processes. The realization of the fact that thinking is not an utterly mysterious process will instill confidence into most pupils and enable them to approach their formal studies with greater zest. Any interest and ingenuity that they may manifest in these drills may be pointed out to them as a sign that they really can think and that future success in studies and in later life will be conditioned chiefly by their faithfulness and perseverance.

DESCRIPTION OF THE DRILLS

First Series, I-1, 2, 3, 4

The first series of drills used in the course is intended to develop the powers of both analysis and invention. Each problem consists of a group of five words, representing five objects or ideas which belong to the same general category, that is, apple, pear, peach, plum, and orange. One member of the group has a quality or qualities which set it off somewhat from the four others. This item should be identified by the pupil and replaced by a new member of the same category that fits more closely with the others. In the above example, the orange is a citrous fruit, and therefore stands out as an intruder among the non-citrous fruits. It should be replaced by cherry, apricot, quince, or some similar fruit which is more akin to the apple, pear, peach, and plum.

Pupils should be trained in this and in other exercises to seek distinctions based upon significant and intrinsic differences, that is, on purpose, nature, function, origin, constituent elements, and so forth. Only in the absence of such important distinctions should they be content with superficial differences based on size, shape, color, texture, location, and so forth. Thus in the above example, to reject peach because it has a pit instead of seeds, or the pear because it is not as round as the others, or the orange because it has a thick skin, would represent superficial thinking.

Second Series, II-1, 2, 3, 4

The objective of the second series of drills is to develop skill in classification. The pupil is presented with groups of ten related words which are to be divided into two sections of five words each. The basis of classification is sometimes rather deep and subtle, sometimes superficial. It may happen in this exercise that the pupil will be totally ignorant of the meaning of one or other of the terms. This, however, should not prevent him from forming a tentative classification based on a process of exclusion. In practical life this is often the only method by which we can solve a problem, yet timid minds often shrink from it as it seems to be a leap in the dark. In the following group: yacht, canoe, skiff, launch, kayak, cruiser, speedboat, rowboat, tug, sampan, it is probable that very few pupils will have heard of the "kayak." This should not deter them from accepting the validity of a classification into "power boats" and "boats propelled by hand." If the pupil has the courage of his conviction that the yacht, launch, cruiser, speedboat and tug are "power boats," and that the canoe, skiff, rowboat and sampan are propelled by hand, he should not hesitate to list the "kayak" in the latter class. He should of course be urged to check this "a priori" reasoning by an appeal to the dictionary.

Third Series, III-1, 2, 3, 4

The third set of drills provides training in the recognition of relationships, one of the most important elements in mental activity. In these exercises the pupil's power to handle relationships is trained by requiring him to supply missing terms in a series of proportions. The process is both analytic and inventive. Analysis is required in recognizing the nature of the relationship that exists between the terms that are given; while invention is exercised in finding a new term that will complete the unfinished proportion. In the initial exercises of this series the pupil is presented with relationships between concrete objects, but gradually he is introduced to relationships between concrete and abstract ideas, thus paving the way for an appreciation of metaphorical language which is more explicitly treated in a later exercise.

Fourth Series, IV-1, 2, 3, 4

A further study in relationships. In these exercises relationships are not merely to be identified in a general way, but they must be named and classified. Each drill consists of thirty-two pairs of nouns which may be related in one of nine different ways. The nine possible relationships are listed at the top of the page, and the pupil is required to select one of these terms as the expression of the relationship existing between the members of each pair of nouns.

Fifth Series, V-1, 2, 3, 4

The first three exercises of this group constitute a test of the pupil's knowledge of words rather than of his thinking power. The drills deal with the recognition of synonyms and antonyms. Emphasis is placed on the need of distinguishing between denotation and connotation. Exercise V-4 deals with the distinction between general and specific terms. Ability to select specific terms is required for effective speech and writing. Skill in selecting a more general term is needed in the process of formulating definitions.

Sixth Series, VI-1, 2, 3, 4

In these drills the student is required to complete a series of statements by supplying missing words. Both analysis and invention are exercised. In the first two drills the statements to be completed are of the nature of definitions. In exercise VI-1 the terms to be defined are concrete; in exercise VI-2 they are abstract. Power in formulating definitions is an important element not only in thinking but in speech and writing as well.

Exercises VI-3 and VI-4 represent a considerable advance over the study of metaphorical language to which pupils were introduced in exercises III-3 and III-4. A series of metaphorical expressions is paralleled by a corresponding series of incompletely formulated proportions. The pupil's task is to analyze the metaphorical sentences, determine the literal meaning, recognize the nature of the relationship that underlies the metaphor, and then supply the missing words in the proportion in such a way that it will form a logical expression of this relationship. It is hoped that these exercises will not only clarify the pupil's thinking by making him conscious of the difference between literal and figurative language, but that it will enhance his appreciation of the literary metaphors that he will meet in his reading. They may even inspire him to greater resourcefulness in introducing a judicious use of metaphor into his own writing.

Supplementary Material

In addition to the six sets of exercises to be used in giving the course, this booklet contains the following supplementary material.

1 A key containing answers to all of the problems.

2 A set of "Topics for Discussion." In these pages the tutor is provided with a quantity of background material which will be of considerable usefulness in planning and conducting the discussions which are an essential element in securing the objectives of the course.

3 A set of "Instructions to Tutors," in which the procedure to be followed is outlined in detail. This includes several pages on "Remedial Work," in which the tutor is instructed how to recognize and correct certain emotional attitudes on the part of his pupils which may interfere with effective thinking.

4 A discussion of "Emotional Obstacles to Clear Thinking." These pages are intended for the use of the pupil. They may be reproduced and copies distributed to the members of the class at the beginning of the course.

5 A brief and simple description of the nature and purposes of the course, addressed directly to the pupils. It is suggested that copies of these pages be given to the members of the class before they assemble for the first meeting.

6 A "Personality Rating Chart" is provided to assist the tutor in judging and recording the reactions of his pupils during the course.

Directions for Exercises I-1, I-2, I-3, and I-4

In each of the following groups, one of the five items belongs to a more or less different category than the other four. Eliminate the disagreeing item and replace it with one that is more closely related to the others. Indicate your reasoning process by completing the explanatory statements that follow: All are . . . Four are . . . One is . . . In computing your score, allow five points for each correct deletion, and five for a suitable replacement. No answer can be considered valid unless it is based on a sound reasoning process.

Example: 1 Apple, pear, peach, plum, ~~orange~~ cherry
All are fruits. Four are non-citrous.
One is citrous.

Exercise I-1

1 Apple, pear, peach, plum, orange
2 Cat, cub, calf, kid, lamb
3 Brass, iron, copper, tin, lead
4 Boil, grill, toast, fry, broil
5 Saw, hammer, plane, chisel, auger
6 Crimson, azure, scarlet, magenta, vermilion
7 Ruby, emerald, sapphire, pearl, garnet
8 Horse, cow, sheep, spaniel, cat
9 Plank, board, joist, lathe, shingle
10 Courageous, staunch, dauntless, ruthless, valiant

Exercise I-2

1 Peony, tulip, canna, lilac, poppy
2 Venison, mutton, beef, veal, bacon
3 Berlin, Paris, New York, Rome, Lisbon
4 Elf, sprite, angel, fairy, gnome
5 Bear, lion, panther, leopard, tiger
6 Gallon, bushel, pound, peck, quart
7 Jefferson, Franklin, Adams, Monroe, Madison
8 Typhoid, cholera, malaria, apoplexy, diphtheria
9 Mason, architect, doctor, lawyer, teacher
10 Sprint, trot, gallop, canter, pace

Exercise I-3

1 Oats, barley, rye, corn, grain
2 Sun, Earth, Jupiter, Saturn, Mars
3 Tortoise, mock-turtle, crab, oyster, lobster
4 Mark, franc, lira, peseta, mill
5 Horse, cow, mule, goat, sheep
6 Biology, botany, astrology, psychology, zoology
7 Nave, choir, transept, crypt, aisle
8 Michigan, Erie, St. Clair, Superior, Huron
9 Radish, potato, beet, cabbage, onion
10 Cloud, mist, mirage, haze, vapor

Exercise I-4

1 Cap, helmet, fez, turban, sombrero
2 Rancid, sour, tart, acrid, pungent
3 Mammoth, colossal, gigantic, herculean, massive
4 Manly, manlike, mannish, manful, virile
5 Timely, quickly, promptly, hastily, speedily
6 Red, black, yellow, green, indigo
7 Gambol, frolic, sport, gamble, frisk
8 Raise, support, lift, elevate, rear
9 Mosaic, etching, fresco, statue, mural
10 Grindstone, sandstone, whetstone, keystone, gravestone

Directions for Exercises II-1, II-2, II-3, and II-4

In each of the following groups, there are two definite classes of objects or ideas. There are five elements in each class. Underline all elements that belong in one of the two classes. In the spaces provided, suggest: 1. a generic term that will describe the whole group; 2. specific terms for the two subdivisions. In computing your score, allow 12 1/2 points for each problem that is solved correctly. A false basis of classification forfeits all credit. If the two classes have been correctly identified, deduct two points for each item that has been improperly listed, and two points for failure to suggest a correct generic term.

Example: 1 <u>Pistol</u>, <u>bow</u>, sword, <u>rifle</u>, club, bowie, axe, <u>cannon</u>, dagger, <u>sling</u>
All are <u>weapons</u>. Five are <u>used for shooting</u>.
Five are <u>used directly on object</u>.

Exercise II-1

1 Pistol, bow, sword, rifle, club, bowie, axe, cannon, dagger, sling
2 Shelf, table, hammock, mantel, bed, davenport, sofa, desk, lounge, escritoire
3 Willow, spruce, sycamore, maple, hemlock, cedar, catalpa, elm, fir, cypress
4 Herd, swarm, horde, crowd, pack, gang, flock, drove, group, clan
5 Hill, lake, estuary, promontory, fiord, dune, prairie, pond, isthmus, lagoon
6 Stomach, heart, kidney, vein, liver, artery, capillary, colon, aorta, spleen
7 Wing, fender, fuselage, tonneau, rudder, brakes, aileron, bumper, chassis, tail
8 Rhine, Amazon, Yukon, Po, Hudson, Ohio, Danube, Nile, Potomac, Tiber

Exercise II-2

1 Bull, ewe, heifer, cock, doe, drake, ram, cow, hen, stag
2 Mountain, defile, mesa, gorge, canyon, glen, cliff, vale, table-land, divide
3 Henry, Richard, Joseph, William, Adam, Louis, David, Benjamin, George, Daniel
4 Marble, tufa, tile, sandstone, brick, porcelain, terra-cotta, granite, stucco, limestone
5 Speed, wheel, motor, power, efficiency, transmission, brakes, differential, style, combustion
6 Mace, mortar, ram, mine, torpedo, catapult, pike, javelin, bomb, shell
7 Pride, arson, greed, larceny, envy, sloth, felony, murder, anger, perjury
8 Pope, Lowell, Byron, Poe, Whittier, Keats, Bryant, Shelley, Milton, Longfellow

Exercise II-3

1 Horse, dog, cow, elephant, lion, bear, giraffe, wolf, tiger, buffalo
2 Organ, violin, piano, trumpet, flute, oboe, guitar, trombone, zither, ukulele
3 Many, countless, small, few, infinitesimal, several, little, great, sundry, big
4 Cotton, wool, leather, silk, alpaca, rubber, fur, linen, straw, rayon

5 Battle, brawl, riot, contest, melee, combat, broil, encounter, affray, skirmish

6 Field, meadow, grove, copse, prairie, forest, moor, steppe, chaparral, thicket

7 Axe, spade, shovel, adze, hammer, plane, rake, scythe, hoe, saw

8 Year, epoch, age, hour, season, minute, era, century, second, moment

Exercise II-4

1 Crow, gull, hawk, lark, thrush, parrot, canary, finch, raven, nightingale

2 When, there, where, hence, henceforth, now, here, then, afterwards, thither

3 Steed, cow, nag, ox, cur, brat, mongrel, boy, man, tramp

4 Cube, square, sphere, triangle, spheroid, pyramid, cone, circle, ellipse, oval

5 Yacht, canoe, skiff, launch, kayak, cruiser, speedboat, rowboat, tug, sampan

6 Bottle, basket, jug, cup, crate, hamper, carafe, carton, sack, demijohn

7 Judge, senator, verdict, bill, governor, veto, writ, lawyer, legislature, jury

8 Brave, brawny, agile, alert, wiry, graceful, ardent, buxom, staunch, polite

Exercise III-1 Supply the missing term in each of the following proportions. Example: Heat is to summer as cold is to winter. Each problem is worth four points.

1 Floor is to house as __________ is to ship.
2 Brush is to painter as __________ is to sculptor.
3 Pound is to sugar as __________ is to gasoline.
4 Mortar is to stone as __________ is to tin.
5 Bell is to church as __________ is to factory.
6 Linoleum is to floor as __________ is to roof.
7 Mile is to journey as __________ is to electricity.
8 Wheel is to wagon as __________ is to sled.
9 Knife is to wood as __________ is to cloth.
10 Bow is to violin as __________ is to ukulele.
11 Glove is to __________ as __________ is to foot.
12 Kennel is to __________ as __________ is to horse.
13 Cat is to __________ as __________ is to rabbit.

14 Mayor is to __________ as __________ is to state.
15 Bank is to __________ as __________ is to ocean.
16 Lion is to __________ as __________ is to birds.
17 Congress is to __________ as __________ is to England.
18 "Out" is to __________ as __________ is to football.
19 Lung is to __________ as __________ is to tree.
20 Sloth is to __________ as __________ is to humility.
21 Cotton is to __________ as __________ is to Minnesota.
22 Quarry is to __________ as __________ is to coal.
23 Wigwam is to __________ as __________ is to Eskimo.
24 Large is to __________ as __________ is to smaller.
25 Dig is to __________ as __________ is to needle.

Exercise III-2

A. Supply the missing terms in each of the following proportions. Example: Heat is to summer as cold is to winter. Each problem is worth five points.

1 Bark is to __________ as __________ is to turtle.
2 Nail is to __________ as __________ is to paw.
3 Egg is to __________ as __________ is to oak.
4 Poetry is to __________ as __________ is to walking.
5 Caterpillar is to __________ as __________ is to frog.
6 Wet is to __________ as __________ is to fire.
7 Wire is to __________ as __________ is to water.
8 Smile is to __________ as __________ is to hate.
9 Herd is to __________ as __________ is to bee.
10 Oval is to __________ as __________ is to square.

B. The following proportions involve a comparison between abstract and concrete ideas. The first and second terms are abstract, the third and fourth are concrete. Example: Variety is to work as spice is to food. The exercise is intended to develop skill in the invention of metaphor.

11 Sorrow is to joy as __________ is to sunshine.
12 Jealousy is to friendship as __________ is to apple.
13 Interest is to capital as __________ is to tree.
14 Effect is to cause as __________ is to fire.
15 Graft is to politics as __________ is to tree.
16 Trouble is to __________ as __________ is to sea.
17 Joy is to __________ as __________ is to machine.

18 Laziness is to __________ as __________ is to bee.
19 Metaphor is to __________ as __________ is to garden.
20 Apology is to __________ as __________ is to wound.

Exercise III-3 In each of the following problems, you are required to find two terms which will be so related to the two which are given that the four taken together can be arranged to form a proportion. The answer to the first problem is: Blue is to sky as green is to grass. Each problem is worth four points.

1 Blue, grass
2 Food, thirst
3 Foot, palm
4 Colt, cow
5 Deep, mountain
6 Leopard, stripes
7 Canoe, oar
8 Hercules, speed
9 Ore, gasoline
10 Electricity, faucet
11 Jazz, language
12 Hence, there
13 Here, then
14 Monk, veil
15 Adverb, noun
16 Horn, locomotive
17 Milk, pound
18 Neither, or
19 Diamond, football
20 Blind, ear
21 Down, in
22 Beef, sheep
23 Airplane, Fulton
24 Apple, wine
25 Mars, wine

Exercise III-4 In each of the following problems, the two terms which are given should suggest two other terms of such nature that they can be combined with the first two to form a proportion. Most of the problems are based on well known natural or conventional symbolism. Each problem is worth four points.

1 Red, "go"
2 Sceptre, crozier
3 Ruddy, illness
4 Speed, ox
5 Minaret, church
6 Sextant, transit
7 Elephant, Democrat
8 Gavel, drum major
9 Lion, fleur-de-lis
10 Oratory, stage
11 Alchemy, astronomy
12 Olive branch, anchor
13 Peacock, wisdom
14 Palace, poverty
15 Cross, crescent
16 Oak, beauty
17 Sheep, stubbornness
18 Spring, old age
19 Cypress, victory
20 Hammer, sickle
21 Egg, arrow
22 Alpha, end
23 Twinkle, dewdrop
24 Ermine, king
25 Milton, drama

Directions for Exercises IV-1, IV-2, IV-3, and IV-4

In each of the following exercises you are presented with thirty-two pairs of words. You are asked to name the relationship that exists between the members of each pair. The required relationships will be expressed by one or another of the nine phrases found at the top of each exercise. In each phrase the significant word is underlined. To indicate the relationship existing between two words in the list, write the proper key word. In computing your score, subtract three points for each error or omission.

Exercise IV-1

1 Is species of	4 Is source of	7 Is purpose of
2 Is cause of	5 Is material of	8 Is based on
3 Is effect of	6 Is same as	9 Is part of

1 Moon . . . tide
2 Bronx . . . New York
3 Tobacco . . . nicotine
4 Terrier . . . dog
5 Immunity . . . vaccination
6 Jealousy . . . quarrel
7 Flour . . . bread
8 Taxes . . . revenue
9 Zebra . . . horse
10 China . . . Orient
11 Politeness . . . culture
12 Spring . . . watch
13 Democracy . . . equality
14 Carbon . . . diamond
15 Division . . . arithmetic
16 Finger . . . hand
17 Branch . . . tree
18 Light . . . fire
19 Reform . . . punishment
20 Cobra . . . snake
21 Education . . . schools
22 Wool . . . felt
23 Credit . . . honesty
24 Oyster . . . pearl
25 Egg . . . albumin
26 South Africa . . . diamonds
27 Earthquake . . . tidal wave
28 Square . . . rectangle
29 Tarantula . . . spider
30 Pneumonia . . . infection
31 Confidence . . . reliability
32 Right to vote . . . citizenship

Exercise IV-2

1 Is source of energy of	4 Is ruler of	7 Is outlet for
2 Is unit of measure of	5 Is index of	8 Is carrier of
3 Is instrument for	6 Is purpose of	9 Is pathway of

1 Scythe . . . reaping
2 Khedive . . . Egypt
3 Air . . . sound
4 Mosquito . . . malaria
5 Horsepower . . . energy
6 Steam . . . locomotive
7 Wrinkles . . . old age
8 Pallor . . . illness
9 Orbit . . . earth
10 Tank car . . . oil

11 Play . . . energy
12 Electricity . . . motor
13 Mile per hour . . . speed
14 Wire . . . electricity
15 Degree . . . heat
16 Chairman . . . assembly
17 Umpire . . . game
18 Volt . . . electrical pressure
19 Gravitation . . . landslide
20 Books . . . information
21 Blushing . . . shame
22 Water . . . typhoid
23 Pore . . . perspiration
24 Ballot . . . voting
25 Channel . . . current
26 Chimney . . . smoke
27 Rivers . . . commerce
28 Lens . . . refraction of light
29 Pound . . . weight
30 Bishop . . . diocese
31 Combustion . . . automobile
32 Pallor . . . fear

Exercise IV-3

1 Is quality of
2 Is similar to
3 Is opposite of
4 Is form of
5 Is accompanied by
6 Is an example of
7 Is equipment for
8 Is prerequisite of
9 Is season for or of

1 Clock . . . watch
2 Storm . . . lightning
3 Winter . . . icicles
4 Bank note . . . money
5 Transparency . . . glass
6 Crab . . . lobster
7 Practice . . . skill
8 Reel . . . fishing
9 Altruism . . . selfishness
10 Tabloid . . . newspaper
11 Industry . . . ant
12 Industry . . . success
13 Zero . . . infinity
14 Racquet . . . tennis
15 Graft . . . dishonesty
16 Create . . . annihilate
17 Mountain . . . valley
18 Arithmetic . . . algebra
19 Horses . . . cavalry
20 Autumn . . . decay
21 Laziness . . . cowardice
22 Pride . . . humility
23 Prosperity . . . high prices
24 August . . . hay fever
25 Bronze . . . brass
26 Courage . . . hero
27 Tennis . . . badminton
28 Ductility . . . gold
29 Microscope . . . research
30 Anger . . . meekness
31 Much . . . little
32 Plasticity . . . putty

Exercise IV-4

1 Is remedy for
2 Is reward for
3 Is model for
4 Is opposite of
5 Is penalty of
6 Is in inverse proportion to
7 Is goal of
8 Is slave to
9 Is analogous to

1 Confiscation . . . smuggling
2 Wing . . . fin
3 Success . . . ambition
4 Agility . . . corpulence
5 Flow of electricity . . . resistance

6 Fur . . . feathers
7 Anesthetic . . . pain
8 Exercise . . . sluggishness
9 Finger . . . toe
10 Drunkard . . . intemperance
11 Unpopularity . . . selfishness
12 Gill . . . lung
13 Discipline . . . disorder
14 Skin . . . bark
15 Specific gravity . . . buoyancy
16 Accuracy . . . haste
17 General . . . admiral
18 Perfection . . . improvement
19 Antiseptic . . . infection
20 Speed . . . burden
21 Oil . . . friction
22 Fish . . . streamlining
23 Visibility . . . haze
24 Failure . . . laziness
25 Target . . . aim
26 Discovery . . . research
27 Island . . . oasis
28 Happiness . . . desire
29 Miser . . . money
30 Purpose . . . destination
31 Prize . . . success
32 Sap . . . blood

Exercise V-1 In the following exercise about one-half of the pairs of words are synonyms, that is, the two words have practically the same meaning. The other pairs are not synonyms and for the most part the two words are unrelated to each other. Place an X on the dotted line after each pair of synonyms. In computing your score, deduct two and one-half points for each mistake.

1 Jump, leap . . . .
2 facade, entrance . . . .
3 altitude, longitude . . . .
4 cut, incision . . . .
5 bury, inter . . . .
6 detonate, explode . . . .
7 affable, sociable . . . .
8 contrive, invent . . . .
9 undermine, annihilate . . . .
10 skull, cranium . . . .
11 ductile, plastic . . . .
12 intestate, insolvent . . . .
13 undulating, rolling . . . .
14 vertex, apex . . . .
15 dilapidated, poorly built . . . .
16 planet, constellation . . . .
17 meteor, constellation . . . .
18 muggy, humid . . . .
19 angry, aggravated . . . .
20 harsh, raucous . . . .
21 censor, blame . . . .
22 molecule, electron . . . .
23 petty, beautiful . . . .
24 sharp, pungent . . . .
25 convex, hollow . . . .
26 reverberate, echo . . . .
27 translucent, transparent . . . .
28 chary, sparing . . . .
29 gentle, timid . . . .
30 curse, swear . . . .
31 clique, faction . . . .
32 pervade, escape . . . .
33 canal, channel . . . .
34 missive, missile . . . .
35 infinite, immeasurable . . . .
36 riddle, enigma . . . .
37 hence, therefore . . . .
38 speed, momentum . . . .
39 perfume, aroma . . . .
40 eldest, oldest . . . .

Exercise V-2 A. In the following exercise, some pairs of words represent ideas which are directly opposed to each other, while other pairs represent ideas which are merely different, that is, they belong to different categories. Opposite ideas must belong to the same category. They may be thought of as occupying positions at the extreme ends of the same line. Go through this list and place an X on the dotted line behind those pairs of ideas which are merely different.

B. All pairs of opposite ideas on this page are so chosen that there is room between them for a middle or a neutral idea. For example, the middle idea between hot and cold is lukewarm. The middle idea between never and always is sometimes. Suggest a middle idea for each pair of true opposites. Write your suggestions on the dotted lines. In computing your score, deduct two points for each false classification and one point for each failure to suggest a proper middle term.

1 red, blue . . . .
2 large, small . . . .
3 cloth, leather . . . .
4 long, short . . . .
5 large, narrow . . . .
6 gold, silver . . . .
7 top, bottom . . . .
8 tree, bush . . . .
9 weak, skillful . . . .
10 ebb, flow . . . .
11 wood, iron . . . .
12 sweet, sour . . . .
13 salt, sugar . . . .
14 rich, bankrupt . . . .
15 forward, backward . . . .
16 love, hate . . . .
17 horse, cow . . . .
18 sailor, soldier . . . .
19 empty, full . . . .
20 knife, fork . . . .
21 football, handball . . . .
22 northeast, southeast . . . .
23 valley, mountain . . . .
24 honored, disgraced . . . .
25 tornado, earthquake . . . .
26 physics, chemistry . . . .
27 nowhere, everywhere. . . .
28 time, space . . . .
29 above, below . . . .
30 assets, liabilities . . . .
31 zenith, nadir . . . .
32 carpet, linoleum . . . .
33 past, future . . . .
34 master, slave . . . .
35 win, lose . . . .
36 larger, smaller . . . .
37 black, white . . . .
38 giant, dwarf . . . .
39 pain, pleasure . . . .
40 right, left . . . .

Exercise V-3 This exercise is a combination of the two preceding members of the series. Some of the pairs of words contain terms of similar meaning, some are made up of opposites, while others comprise words which are neither similar nor opposite, that is, they belong to different categories. Indicate pairs of similar terms by placing an S on the dotted line. Mark pairs of opposite terms with an O, and place an N after those pairs in which the words are neither similar nor opposite. Deduct two points for each incorrect response.

1 levity, frivolity . . .
2 sight, vision . . .
3 tranquil, tempestuous . . .
4 create, annihilate . . .
5 parallel, equal . . .
6 inception, conclusion . . .
7 ocular, auditory . . .
8 parlor, salon . . .
9 carnivorous, voracious . . .
10 empirical, imperious . . .
11 loquacious, taciturn . . .
12 rodent, ruminant . . .
13 dilate, delete . . .
14 saline, salty . . .
15 farmer, mechanic . . .
16 carnation, incarnation . . .
17 enslave, subjugate . . .
18 longitude, altitude . . .
19 harmony, concord . . .
20 longevity, heredity . . .
21 heavy, ponderous . . .
22 moon, satellite . . .
23 microscopic, infinitesimal . . .
24 exaggerate, minimize . . .
25 volatile, voluminous . . .
26 pace, step . . .
27 infinite, limitless . . .
28 transient, frequent . . .
29 opaque, translucent . . .
30 callous, fibrous . . .
31 vibrate, oscillate . . .
32 dense, sparse . . .
33 condemn, acquit . . .
34 independent, autonomous . . .
35 wavy, undulating . . .
36 squirm, writhe . . .
37 bliss, woe . . .
38 fume, fumigate . . .
39 reimburse, repay . . .
40 call, summon . . .
41 transparent, luminous. . .
42 vilify, extol . . .
43 refine, purify . . .
44 victorious, neutral . . .
45 simple, compound . . .
46 complex, complicated. . .
47 moonlight, twilight . . .
48 solid, stolid . . .
49 indemnify, redeem . . .
50 henchman, satellite . . .

Exercise V-4 This exercise deals with the distinction between general and specific terms. In Part A the three words in each group are arranged alphabetically. Rearrange these words in such a way that the most general word will come first and the most specific word will be last. Indicate your arrangement by writing the numbers 1, 2, and 3 over the proper words. The first group should be numbered as follows: 1 garment, 2 coat, 3 ulster. The reasoning process runs as follows: Every coat is a garment, but not every garment is a coat. Therefore, coat is a more specific word than garment. Deduct two points for each mistake.

Part A

1 coat, garment, ulster
2 filly, horse, mare
3 joist, lumber, wood
4 air, fluid, gas
5 gas, steam, vapor
6 fodder, food, hay
7 bird, falcon, hawk
8 cobra, reptile, snake
9 beagle, dog, hound
10 chair, rocker, seat
11 boat, cruiser, ship
12 address, oration, panegyric
13 contest, marathon, race
14 fresco, mural, painting
15 box, casket, chest
16 beaver, mammal, rodent
17 currency, money, specie
18 burn, cremate, oxidize
19 base, bottom, foundation
20 building, church, edifice

Part B Suggest a more specific term for each of the following:

1 soldier . . . .
2 gun . . . .
3 fat . . . .
4 Oriental . . . .
5 red . . . .
6 sword . . . .
7 field . . . .
8 virtue . . . .
9 house . . . .
10 side . . . .
11 road . . . .
12 tooth . . . .

Part C Suggest a more general term for each of the following:

1 cyclone . . . .
2 rye . . . .
3 petroleum . . . .
4 broth . . . .
5 Breton . . . .
6 tome . . . .
7 gondola . . . .
8 pennant . . . .
9 epic . . . .
10 dromedary . . . .
11 creek . . . .
12 metropolis . . . .

Exercise VI-1 A definition is an explanation in a single sentence of the meaning of a word or term. The predicate of a definition contains two parts: 1 A word or phrase which gives the general classification of the idea or object denoted by the word which is being defined. 2 One or more words or phrases which serve to distinguish the object or idea from all other members of its class. In the following examples, the underlined words give the general classification, and the words which follow give the specific difference.

A table is an article of furniture having a smooth, flat top fixed on legs.

A razor is a keen-edged instrument used for shaving the beard.

You are asked to complete the definitions given below by writing the proper word in each of the vacant spaces. Use only one word in each space. When you have supplied all the missing words, draw a line under the word or phrase in each definition which gives the general classification. In computing your score, deduct two points for each mistake.

1 A river is a natural __________ of __________ larger than a __________.

2 A chair is a movable single __________ having a __________ and usually supported by four __________.

3 A square is a plane __________ having __________ equal __________ and __________ right __________.

4 A __________ is a dagger-like instrument __________ to the muzzle of a __________.

5 A __________ is a cup-shaped metallic __________ which __________ forth a ringing __________ on being struck with a __________.

6 A balloon is a nonporous __________ filled with a __________ lighter than __________ which enables it to __________ from the __________ and __________ in the atmosphere.

7 A bicycle is a light __________ having two __________, one __________ the other and propelled by the __________ acting on __________.

8 __________ is the life-sustaining __________ which circulates in the heart, __________ and __________ of an __________.

9 A __________ is a weapon constructed of a strip of __________ material and used to propel __________ by the resilient action of a __________ which connects its two __________.

10 A spy is a __________ who secretly __________ information about an __________ resources and plans for use by his own __________.

Exercise VI-2 Complete the definitions given below by filling in the vacant spaces. Use only one word for each space. When you have supplied all of the missing words, draw a line under the word or phrase in each definition which gives the general classification of the idea which is being defined. In computing your score, deduct two points for each mistake.

1 Murder is the deliberate and unlawful __________ of a __________ being.

2 __________ is __________ measured leaping or stepping to the __________ of music or rhythmic beats.

3 Envy is a sense of __________ aroused by the thought of another's __________.

4 Slavery is the __________ of being involuntarily __________ to __________ will.

5 Auction is the public __________ of property to the __________ bidder.

6 __________ is the science and art that deals __________ the __________, cure or alleviation of __________.

7 Treason is the __________ of attempting by overt act to overthrow the government of the __________ to __________ the offender owes __________.

8 A duel is a prearranged __________ between __________ persons, fought with lethal __________ usually in the __________ of witnesses known as __________.

9 Biology is the __________ which treats of the origin, development and function of __________ and __________.

10 __________ is an act by which a rational __________ acknowledges the __________ power and excellence of the __________.

11 A metaphor is a __________ of __________ which suggests a resemblance __________ two objects by applying to __________ an expression which in a __________ sense belongs only to the __________.

12 Equilibrium is a __________ of balance __________ opposing __________.

Exercise VI-3 This exercise calls for an analysis of metaphorical language. The metaphor in each problem is to be reduced to the form of a proportion. Record your solutions by filling out the formulae that follow the problems. Put only one word in each space. Before attempting to construct a proportion, make sure that you understand the exact meaning that underlies the figurative language of the problem sentence. In computing your score, allow four points for each blank that has been correctly filled.

1 Hard work is the key to success.	Hard work is to success as ________ is to treasure chest.
2 His heart is bigger than his head.	Heart is to ________ as ________ is to prudence.
3 Do not hide your light under a bushel.	Bushel basket is to ________ as ________ modesty is to ________.
4 Success always goes to his head.	________ is to pride as ________ is to intoxication.
5 He looked at the world with jaundiced eye.	Envy is to the mind as ________ vision is to the ________.

6	His reputation was un-tarnished.	Suspicion is to ________ as ________ lustre is to precious metal.
7	His laughter disinfected the morbid atmosphere.	________ is to gloom as ________ is to germ-laden ________.
8	The debater's rebuttal was wide of the mark.	Inept ________ is to opponent's ________ as ill-aimed ________ is to ________.
9	The tourists drank in the beauty of the scene.	Scenic ________ is to the eye as delicious ________ is to the lips and ________.
10	Next day the once proud battleship limped piti-fully into port.	________ navigation is to damaged ________ as limping ________ is to ________ animal.

Exercise VI-4 This exercise calls for an analysis of metaphorical language. The metaphor in each problem is to be reduced to the form of a proportion. Record your solution by filling out the formulae that follow the problems. Put only one word in each space. Before attempting to construct a proportion, make sure that you understand the exact meaning that underlies the figurative language of the problem sentence. In computing your score, allow three points for each blank that has been correctly filled.

1	He dipped each word in deadly sarcasm.	________ is to speech as ________ is to a savage warrior's ________.
2	He marshalled his ar-guments with Napoleonic strategy.	Clever choice and ________ of arguments is to ________ as ________ is to warfare.
3	The pall of atheism lay heavy on the land.	________ is to souls of men as ________ is to a corpse.
4	He zoomed into his sub-ject with a burst of eloquence.	Burst of eloquence is to ________ as ________ under ________ power is to aviator.
5	He tried to parry the rapier thrusts of his clever opponent with the bludgeon of per-sonal abuse.	Subtle ________ is to ________ lan-guage as ________ is to heavy ________.
6	He tried to enliven his anemic style with the rouge of figurative language.	Flowery ________ is to dearth of ________ as ________ is to pallid ________.
7	His library was a liter-ary catacomb.	________ is to unused books as an underground ________ is to the ________ of the dead.

8 Many a noble character has been cradled in poverty.	________ is to early education as ________ is to ________.
9 The north wind whirled the fallen leaves into a carnival of frenzied dancing.	________ motion is to fallen ________ as wild ________ is to ________ guests at a ________.
10 The flotsam and jetsam of chaotic memories whirled and drifted through his mind.	Disconnected ________ are to an excited ________ as floating ________ is to the surface of a ________ sea.

KEY TO EXERCISES

	Delete	Insert	All Are	Four Are	One Is
Exercise I-1					
1	orange	cherry	fruits	non-citrous	citrous
2	cat	kitten	animals	young	full grown
3	brass	zinc	metals	simple	alloy
4	boil	roast	ways of cooking	without water	with water
5	hammer	hatchet	tools	for cutting	for striking
6	azure	Indian red	colors	kinds of red	blue
7	pearl	diamond	precious stones	minerals	of animal origin
8	spaniel	dog	animals	generic	specific
9	lathe	lath	no common class	wood for building	machine for turning
10	ruthless	brave	adjectives	favorable	unfavorable
Exercise I-2					
1	lilac	aster	plants	herbs	shrub
2	bacon	pork	meats	not processed	processed
3	New York	Madrid	large cities	European capitals	American metropolis
4	angel	nymph	spirits	mythical	real
5	bear	jaguar	wild animals	cats	not a cat
6	pound	pint	units of measure	by volume	by weight
7	Franklin	Washington	statesmen	presidents	diplomat
8	apoplexy	pneumonia	diseases	germ diseases	bursting of artery
9	mason	journalist	avocations	professions	a trade
10	sprint	amble	gaits	used of horses	not used of horses

Exercise I-3

1	grain	wheat	grains	specific	generic
2	Sun	Venus	members of solar system	planets	central body
3	mock turtle	turtle	hard-shelled animals	real	fictitious
4	mill	dollar	money	coined	not coined
5	mule	donkey	domestic animals	true species	hybrid
6	astrology	astronomy	sciences	true sciences	pseudoscience
7	crypt	sanctuary	parts of a church	above ground	below ground
8	St. Clair	Ontario	Great Lakes	large	small
9	cabbage	carrot	vegetables	edible bulbs	edible leaf only
10	mirage	fog	atmospheric phenomena	suspended matter	optical illusion

Exercise I-4

1	helmet	hat	headgear	civilian	military
2	rancid	bitter	sharp tastes	natural	due to spoiling
3	herculean	large	adjectives	denoting size	denoting strength
4	mannish	masculine	adjectives	applied to men favorably	applied to women unfavorably
5	timely	instantly	-ly words	adverbs	adjective
6	black	orange	colors	prismatic	absence of color
7	gamble	play	diversions	without stakes	with stakes
8	support	hoist	resistance to gravity	movements	without movement
9	statue	painting	works of art	two dimensional	three dimensional
10	sandstone	milestone	stones	functional names	named from material

N.B. It is to be noted that this key does not contain all possible correct answers.

KEY TO EXERCISES

All Are	Five Are	Five Are
Exercise II-1		
1 weapons	used for shooting	used directly on object
2 furniture	for persons	for inanimate objects
3 trees	evergreen	deciduous
4 collective nouns	for animals only	for men
5 geographical features	water	land
6 organs of body	for blood circulation	abdominal organs
7 parts of vehicles	airplane parts	automobile parts
8 rivers	in Eastern Hemisphere	in Western Hemisphere
Exercise II-2		
1 animals	males	females
2 topographical features	elevations	depressions
3 masculine names	biblical	nonbiblical
4 stones	natural	artificial
5 motor terms	abstract	concrete
6 weapons	ancient (nonexplosive)	modern (explosive)
7 sinful habits or acts	sinful habits or moods	criminal acts
8 poets	American	English

Exercise II-3

1 animals	carnivorous	herbivorous
2 musical instruments	wind instruments	string instruments
3 adjectives	number	size
4 materials for clothing	from plants	from animals
5 conflicts	disorderly	honorable
6 landscape divisions	wooded	treeless
7 tools	for carpentry	for gardening and so forth
8 periods of time	of definite length	of indefinite length

Exercise II-4

1 birds	songsters	not songsters
2 adverbs	of time	of place
3 living beings	favorable terms	derogatory terms
4 geometric figures	plane	solid
5 small craft	propelled by hand	propelled by engine or wind
6 containers	for liquids	for nonliquids
7 civil terms	judicial	legislative
8 adjectives	mental qualities	physical qualities

KEY TO EXERCISES

Exercise III-1

1 deck; 2 chisel; 3 gallon; 4 solder; 5 whistle; 6 tile, shingles, and so forth; 7 volt, kilowatt, and so forth; 8 runner; 9 scissors; 10 pick; 11 hand, shoe; 12 dog, stable; 13 mouse, dog; 14 city, governor; 15 river, shore; 16 animals, eagle; 17 United States, Parliament; 18 baseball, "down"; 19 animal, leaf; 20 diligence, pride; 21 Alabama, wheat; 22 stone, mine; 23 Indian, igloo; 24 larger, small; 25 spade, sew.

Exercise III-2

1 tree, shell; 2 hand, claw; 3 chicken, acorn; 4 prose, dancing; 5 butterfly, tadpole; 6 water, hot; 7 electricity, pipe; 8 love, scowl; 9 cow, swarm; 10 circle, oblong; 11 darkness; 12 worm; 13 fruit; 14 smoke; 15 parasite vine; 16 life, storm; 17 work, oil; 18 diligence, drone (or, drone, diligence); 19 style, flower; 20 insult, salve.

Exercise III-3

1 blue : sky :: green : grass
2 food : hunger :: drink : thirst
3 sole : foot :: palm : hand
4 calf : cow :: colt : horse
5 deep : valley :: high : mountain
6 spots : leopard :: stripes : zebra
7 paddle : canoe :: oar : rowboat
8 Hercules : strength :: Mercury : speed
9 ore : iron :: petroleum : gasoline
10 switch : electricity :: faucet : water
11 jazz : music :: slang : language
12 hence : here :: thence : there
13 here : there :: now : then
here : now :: then : there
14 cowl : monk :: veil : nun
15 adjective : noun :: adverb : verb
16 horn : automobile :: whistle : locomotive
17 quart : milk :: pound : butter
18 neither : nor :: either : or
neither : either :: nor : or
19 diamond : baseball :: gridiron : football
20 blind : eye :: deaf : ear
21 up : down :: in : out

22 beef : steer :: mutton : sheep
23 Wright Brothers : airplane :: Fulton : steamboat
24 apple : cider :: grape : wine
25 Mars : war :: Bacchus : wine

Exercise III-4

1 red : "stop" :: green : "go"
2 sceptre : king :: crosier : bishop
3 ruddy : health :: pale : illness
4 speed : deer :: strength : ox
5 minaret : mosque :: steeple : church
6 sextant : sailor :: transit : surveyor
7 elephant : Republican :: donkey : Democrat
8 gavel : chairman :: baton : drum major
9 lion : England :: fleur-de-lis : France
10 platform : oratory :: stage : drama
11 alchemy : chemistry :: astrology : astronomy
12 olive branch : peace :: anchor : hope
13 peacock : pride :: owl : wisdom
14 palace : wealth :: hovel : poverty
15 Cross : Christianity :: crescent : Mohammedanism
16 oak : strength :: rose : beauty
17 stupidity : sheep :: stubbornness : mule
18 spring : youth :: autumn : old age
19 cypress : mourning :: laurel : victory
20 hammer : industry :: sickle : farming
21 egg : life :: arrow : death
22 alpha : beginning :: omega : end
23 twinkle : star :: sparkle : dewdrop
24 ermine : judge :: purple : king
25 Milton : epic :: Shakespeare : drama

Exercise IV-1

1 cause
2 part
3 source
4 species
5 purpose
6 source, cause
7 material
8 source
9 species
10 part
11 part, effect
12 part
13 based
14 material
15 part
16 part
17 part
18 effect
19 purpose
20 species
21 purpose
22 material
23 based
24 source
25 source
26 source
27 cause
28 species
29 species
30 species, effect
31 based
32 based

Exercise IV-2

1	instrument	12	energy	23	outlet
2	ruler	13	measure	24	instrument
3	carrier	14	carrier, pathway	25	pathway
4	carrier	15	measure	26	outlet
5	measure	16	ruler	27	pathway
6	energy	17	ruler	28	instrument
7	index	18	measure	29	measure
8	index	19	energy	30	ruler
9	pathway	20	carrier	31	energy
10	carrier	21	index	32	index
11	outlet	22	carrier		

Exercise IV-3

1	similar	12	prerequisite	23	accompanied
2	accompanied	13	opposite	24	season
3	season	14	equipment	25	similar
4	form	15	form	26	quality
5	quality	16	opposite	27	similar
6	similar	17	opposite	28	quality
7	prerequisite	18	prerequisite	29	equipment
8	equipment	19	equipment	30	opposite
9	opposite	20	season	31	opposite
10	form	21	form	32	quality
11	quality	22	opposite		

Exercise IV-4

1	penalty	12	analogous	23	inverse
2	analogous	13	remedy, opposite	24	penalty
3	goal	14	analogous	25	goal
4	inverse	15	inverse	26	goal
5	inverse	16	inverse	27	analogous
6	analogous	17	analogous	28	goal
7	remedy	18	goal	29	slave
8	remedy	19	remedy	30	analogous
9	analogous	20	inverse	31	reward
10	slave	21	remedy	32	analogous
11	penalty	22	model		

Exercise V-1

Synonyms: 1, 4, 5, 6, 7, 8, 10, 13, 14, 18, 20, 24, 26, 28, 31, 35, 36, 37, 39, 40

Exercise V-2

Middle terms for true opposites:

2	medium	19	half full	33	present
4	medium	23	plain	34	partner
7	middle	24	unknown	35	break even
10	turn of tide	27	somewhere	36	equal
12	insipid	29	on level with	37	gray
14	merely solvent	30	things of no value	38	normal man
15	stationary	31	horizon, or position of observer	39	insensibility
16	indifference			40	center

Exercise V-3

Synonyms: 1, 2, 8, 14, 17, 19, 21, 22, 23, 26, 27, 31, 34, 35, 36, 39, 40, 43, 46, 50

Opposites: 3, 4, 6, 11, 24, 29, 32, 33, 37, 42, 45

Exercise V-4, Part A

1	garment, coat, ulster	11	boat, ship, cruiser
2	horse, mare, filly	12	address, oration, panegyric
3	wood, lumber, joist	13	contest, race, marathon
4	fluid, gas, air	14	painting, mural, fresco
5	gas, vapor, steam	15	box, chest, casket
6	food, fodder, hay	16	mammal, rodent, beaver
7	bird, hawk, falcon	17	money, currency, specie
8	reptile, snake, cobra	18	oxidize, burn, cremate
9	dog, hound, beagle	19	bottom, base, foundation
10	seat, chair, rocker	20	building, edifice, church

Exercise V-4, Part B

1	marine	4	Chinese	7	meadow	10	flank
2	rifle	5	crimson	8	courage	11	highway
3	obese	6	rapier	9	cottage	12	molar

Exercise V-4, Part C

1	storm	4	soup	7	boat	10	camel
2	grain	5	Frenchman	8	flag	11	stream
3	oil	6	book	9	poem	12	city

Exercise VI-1

1 A river is a natural stream of water larger than a creek.

2 A chair is a movable single seat having a back and usually supported by four legs.

3 A square is a plane figure having four equal sides and four right angles.

4 A bayonet is a dagger-like instrument fitted to the muzzle of a rifle.

5 A bell is a cup-shaped metallic vessel which gives forth a ringing sound on being struck with a hammer (clapper).

6 A balloon is a nonporous bag filled with a gas lighter than air which enables it to rise from the ground and float in the atmosphere.

7 A bicycle is a light vehicle having two wheels, one behind the other, and propelled by the feet acting on pedals.

8 Blood is the life-sustaining fluid which circulates in the heart, arteries and veins of an animal.

9 A bow is a weapon constructed of a strip of elastic material and used to propel arrows by the resilient action of a string which connects its two ends.

10 A spy is a person who secretly obtains information about an opponent's resources and plans for use by his own party.

Exercise VI-2

1 Murder is the deliberate and unlawful killing of a human being.

2 Dancing is a measured stepping or leaping to the accompaniment of music or rhythmic beats.

3 Envy is a sense of sadness aroused by the thought of another's success.

4 Slavery is the state of being involuntarily subject to another's will.

5 Auction is the public sale of property to the highest bidder.

6 Medicine is the science and art that deals with the prevention, cure, or alleviation of disease.

7 Treason is the crime of attempting by overt act to overthrow the government of the country to which the offender owes allegiance.

8 A duel is a prearranged combat between two persons, fought with lethal weapons, usually in the presence of witnesses known as seconds.

9 Biology is the science which treats of the origin, development, and function of plants and animals.

10 Worship is an act by which a rational being acknowledges the supreme power and excellence of the Deity.

11 A metaphor is a figure of speech which suggests a resemblance between two objects by applying to one an expression which in a strict sense belongs only to the other.

12 Equilibrium is a state of balance between opposing forces.

Exercise VI-3

1 Hard work is to success as key is to treasure chest.
2 Heart is to generosity as head is to prudence.
3 Bushel basket is to candle as false modesty is to talent.
4 Success is to pride as wine is to intoxication.
5 Envy is to the mind as yellow vision is to the eye.
6 Suspicion is to reputation as tarnished luster is to precious metal.
7 Laughter is to gloom as disinfectant is to germ-laden atmosphere.
8 Inept rebuttal is to opponent's argument as ill-aimed arrow is to target.
9 Scenic beauty is to the eye and mind as delicious beverage is to lips and throat.
10 Difficult navigation is to damaged battleship as limping gait is to wounded animal.

Exercise VI-4

1 Sarcasm is to speech as poison is to a savage warrior's arrow.
2 Clever choice and arrangement of arguments is to debate as strategy is to warfare.
3 Atheism is to souls of men as pall is to a corpse.
4 Burst of eloquence is to orator as ascent under full power is to aviator.
5 Subtle argument is to abusive language as rapier is to heavy club.
6 Flowery language is to dearth of ideas as rouge is to pallid features.
7 Library is to unused books as underground cemetery is to bodies of the dead.
8 Poverty is to early education as cradle is to infant.
9 Whirling motion is to fallen leaves as wild dancing is to over-excited guests at a carnival.
10 Disconnected memories are to an excited mind as floating debris is to surface of a stormy sea.

TOPICS FOR DISCUSSION

Exercise I-1

1 Citrous fruits have heavy outer rinds, cellular pulp arranged in sections, and a characteristic acid taste, due to the presence of some form of citric acid. Other citrous fruits are the lemon, grapefruit, lime, tangerine, kumquat, mandarine, and citron. Apples and pears are called "pome" fruits. To reject the plum because it is smaller than the others, or the peach, because it has a fuzzy skin, represents superficial thinking. Nectarines are peaches with a smooth skin, similar to the skin of the plum. The nectarine is not a cross between the peach and the plum.

2 To reject "cub" because it is a wild animal is not a very good solution, for when we speak of wild animals, we usually refer to the adults. What are the skins of some of these animals used for?

3 Zinc would be a good substitute for brass because it is suggested by brass which is an alloy of copper and zinc. Pupils should be instructed to make the minimum change which will bring the intruding element into line with the others. An alloy is a union of two metals, but the word is also applied to the union of a metal with a nonmetal. For example, steel is an alloy of iron and carbon. Bronze is a combination of copper and tin. Bronze is used in art; brass is used in industry.

4 "Toast" may be rejected because it is a method of treating bread, while the other operations are used in cooking meat. In broiling, the fire is above the meat; in grilling, it is below.

5 An auger is a spiral drill for making holes in wood, although large augers are used for drilling post holes. Even if the pupils do not know the meaning of "auger," they should be able to solve this problem by the method of exclusion. This is the reasoning process: We must have a four to one division. Now saws, planes, and chisels are cutting tools, while the hammer is not. This gives us a three to one division. Hence it would be a very good conjecture to class the auger with the cutting tools. Of course this conjecture should be verified later by an appeal to the dictionary.

6 To replace azure with the general word "red" is not as good an answer as to substitute a more specific term, that is, Chinese

red, since the other terms are specific.

7 Pupils should be asked how pearls are formed in the oyster shell. A grain of sand enters the shell and irritates the oyster. The oyster cannot remove it, so it covers it with a slimy deposit which hardens into a pearl. Pearls are produced artificially by placing grains of sand in oyster shells. Mother of pearl, or nacre, is the pearly lining of the oyster shell. Ask for the colors of the other stones.

8 To class these items as animals is correct, but "domestic animals" is a better term.

9 This problem contains a trick, Pupils will misread "lath" for "lathe." A lathe is a machine for the shaping of cylindrical objects in metal or wood. In the use of the lathe, the material is moved, while the tool remains more or less stationary. Analogous to the lathe is the potter's wheel. A joist is a heavy timber used to support the planks in a floor. A plank is a thin piece of timber used for surfacing. Take occasion to point out that a final silent "e" makes the preceding vowel long, that is, met, mete; writ, write; not, note; cut, cute, and so forth.

10 These adjectives express aggressive qualities, though "staunch" is often applied to a brave defender. "Staunch" is more commonly spelled "stanch." The two spellings have the same pronunciation, that is, to rhyme with "branch," not with "launch."

Exercise I-2

1 A shrub is a plant with a woody stem smaller than a tree. It may also be a vine or a bush. A bush is a plant with a number of small woody stems. A herb is a plant not having a woody stem. Poppy may be deleted on the score that it is cultivated as the source of opium. Opium is the juice of the poppy thickened by evaporation. Morphine is an alkaloid derivative of opium. Other derivatives of opium are heroin and codein, the former very strong, the latter comparatively weak. These drugs are used in medicine to alleviate pain. Used injudiciously they are habit forming.

2 Venison may be rejected for the reason that it is the flesh of an undomesticated animal.

3 Washington would be a correct substitute for New York, but Madrid is better as the other cities are European capitals.

4 An elf is the same as a sprite. Gnomes were supposed to be the guardians of caves and mines. Fairies are associated with forests and fields, and were supposed to meddle in human affairs. Other mythical beings are pixies, mermen and mermaids.

5 Pupils should be asked to give a number of substitutes for bear, such as cougar, puma, jaguar, and so forth. A cat is a carnivorous quadruped, which stealthily approaches its prey, crouches, springs, and alights on the back of its victim. Pupils should note that definitions of animals are descriptive rather than essential.

6 The quart is both a wet and a dry measure. Some pupils may wrongly maintain that the peck is a measure by weight, for they have seen grocers, for the sake of convenience, weigh out a peck of potatoes.

7 To substitute a recent president for Franklin would be correct but not desirable, since the other presidents in the list belong to our early history.

8 Malaria means "bad air." This disease was falsely believed to be caused by an unwholesome climate, especially by night air. We now know that it is caused by the bite of the anopheles mosquito which flies only after sundown.

9 A profession is a calling in which broad learning is more important than manual skill and in which the subject matter is mental and cultural rather than utilitarian. On the other hand, the term "professional" is applied to one who pursues as a business an activity which is engaged in by others as a pastime or hobby, that is, any sport.

10 It is rather difficult to give an accurate description of the various gaits of a horse. (See illustrations under "movement" in large Standard Dictionary.) The following brief discussion may be of use.

In galloping the horse springs into the air from a fore foot and lands on the diagonal hind foot. If he springs from the right fore foot, the feet return to the ground in this order: left hind foot, right hind foot, left fore foot, right fore foot. At the high point in the leap all four legs are flexed beneath the body, the hind feet being ahead of the fore feet.

The canter is an easy form of the gallop. This was the favorite pace used by pilgrims on their way to the shrine of Thomas a Becket at Canterbury, hence the origin of the term. In trotting the horse uses his legs in diagonal pairs, and in pacing the legs are paired laterally, that is, in right and left pairs. In both of these movements the horse is entirely unsupported twice during each complete stride. Walking and ambling are very similar. In the former the horse is always supported by two or three feet, in the latter by one or two. In both gaits the feet touch the ground in the same order, that is, RFF, LHF, LFF, RHF.

Exercise I-3

1 In the Old World, the word corn is applied to any kind of grain, while in the New World it usually denotes what is known as maize, or Indian Corn.

2 Pupils should be asked to distinguish between planets and stars. Stars are really suns which shine by their own light; while a planet is a relatively cold body which revolves around a sun. Stars twinkle, while planets do not. A satellite is a secondary planet, that is, a celestial body that revolves around a planet. Our satellite is called the moon. Jupiter has four moons; Saturn has a luminous ring. Mars is the only planet in our system that seems capable of supporting life as we know it.

3 The distinction between tortoise, turtle, and terrapin is not very definite. However, "turtle" is the most general word and includes all the others. "Tortoise" is applied mainly to land turtles, while the "terrapin," generally speaking, is a fresh-water turtle.

4 The mill is not an actual coin. It is a unit of value, equal to one-tenth of a cent, and is used for convenience in computing taxes, and so forth. Such units are called "money of account." Before the first World War, the French franc, the Spanish peseta, and the Italian lira were of equal value, a fraction over 19¢. The German mark was practically the same in value as the English shilling, that is, about 24¢.

5 A mule is a hybrid animal, a cross between the donkey and a horse. Mules are bred by crossing a male donkey with a mare. Mules are sterile.

6 Biology is a general term and includes botany and zoology. However, it would not be a good word to delete here, since astrology is much more out of line. Astrology is a pseudoscience of great antiquity usually associated with the Babylonians, who thought that they could tell a person's fortune by computing the position of the stars on the day when he was born. An astrologer's prediction is known as a horoscope. In one sense, astrology is the mother of modern astronomy; just as alchemy is the mother of modern chemistry.

7 The crypt was originally a burial vault beneath a church. The term is now applied to a basement chapel. In modern churches the choir is usually a balcony in the rear of the church for the use of singers, but in monastic churches the choir is immediately in front of the sanctuary, for it is in that part of the church that the monks chant the Divine Office. In a cruciform church the choir is that portion which lies between the transept and the altar. Architecturally, an aisle is that part of a church which is separated from the nave by a row of columns. The term is commonly applied to the open space between rows of pews.

8 While Lake St. Clair is a true member of the chain of Great Lakes, it is too small to hold a place on our list against Lake Ontario. These lakes constitute the largest expanse of fresh water in the world.

9 Beet greens may be eaten, but this does not vitiate our distinction, since the bulb is the more valuable part of the beet.

10 A brief explanation of "mirage" may be given here. A mirage is due to the reflection of a distant object in a natural mirror, formed by the dividing line between two layers of air of different temperatures. There are two kinds of mirages: (1) When the mirrored surface is close to the ground and therefore beneath the eye, it may reflect the clouds in the sky and give the thirsty traveler the impression that a lake lies ahead. (2) When the mirror surface is high in the atmosphere and therefore above the eye, it may reflect distant objects which are on the earth's surface; such as, buildings, or a ship at sea. Such images are usually in-

verted. Haze may be due to smoke, as well as to moisture. Mist always connotes moisture. Vapor is the gaseous form of a substance which, at ordinary temperatures, is a solid or a liquid.

Exercise I-4

1 The fez is the national headgear of the Turks. It is a round cap, usually red, carrying a tassel. The turban, much used by Mohammedans, is a cap with a scarf wound around it.

2 Rancidity usually implies spoiling, but sourness is often a natural quality. Tartness is a more or less agreeable sharpness; acridity is sharp and harsh; pungency, which is very sharp, is applied to both taste and smell.

3 The mammoth was a very large elephant, now extinct. Colossus was a name given by the Greeks to any huge statue. The most famous example was the Colossus of Rhodes, a bronze statue of Apollo, over one hundred feet high. It was destroyed by an earthquake about two hundred years before Christ. Hercules was a mythical Greek hero famous for his strength.

4 The suffix "-ish," when added to nouns, has an unfavorable connotation, except in the case of national names, such as, "Turkish." With adjectives, this suffix has the force of "somewhat," that is, "bluish." The suffix "-ly" may be considered a short form of "like."

5 Call attention to the fact that when the suffix "-ly" is added to a noun it produces an adjective: when added to an adjective, it produces an adverb.

6 In a scientific sense, black is not a true color. It is rather the absence of color. The seven primary colors are red, orange, yellow, green, blue, indigo, and violet. Sunlight, which is white, is a mixture of these colors. The color of any given material is determined by the elements of sunlight which are reflected from its surface. The other rays are absorbed. Pure snow is white because it reflects all of the sun's rays. In the visible spectrum the red rays are longest, the violet rays are shortest. Ultra-violet rays, which are the cause of sunburn, are too short to be perceived by the eye. Infrared rays, closely akin to heat rays, are too long to be perceived by the eye. The infrared camera can take pictures through a fog which obstructs ordinary vision.

8 The word "raise" should not be used to signify the upbringing of children. We raise cattle and crops, but we rear a family.

9 A mosaic is a surface decoration or picture made by inlaying small, colored stones, and so forth. An etching is a design cut into a metallic surface by the use of acids. A wood etching is a design burned into the surface of wood by means of a hot needle. A fresco is a picture or design painted on fresh, that is, wet plaster.

10 This problem illustrates a very important distinction in the use of names. Pupils should be asked to suggest names of objects based on function, material, shape, origin, location, and so forth. For example, among golf clubs we have the putter and driver as functional names; the brassie and midiron as names based on material; the spoon, so called from its original shape. Most pupils will not know the meaning of keystone. It should be explained by a diagram. It is the central stone in an arch, which frequently projects beyond the others and is sometimes decorated.

Exercise II-1

1 These weapons may be classed as ancient and modern, although this answer is not as good as the distinction between projectile-throwing weapons and percussion weapons. The bowie is a long, curved knife, named after its inventor, Colonel Bowie, who lived at the beginning of the last century. Some pupils will think that "sling" is the same as slingshot. A sling is a leather socket to which two strings are attached, one on either side. A round missile, made of stone or metal, is placed in the socket and whirled rapidly around the head until it attains sufficient velocity. It is then dispatched by the sudden release of one of the strings. Recall the story of David and Goliath.

2 An escritoire is a small writing desk, also called a secretary.

3 Discuss the difference between deciduous and coniferous, or evergreen trees. One has leaves, the other needles. However some evergreen trees have leaves, that is, the laurel and the cypress. There are two kinds of maple--hard and soft. Maple syrup comes from the hard maple. Hard maple is used for flooring; cedar is used for moth-proof cabinets, and also for posts, because it does not rot in the ground. The cypress tree among the ancients was a symbol of mourning. It was frequently planted near tombs.

4 Pupils should be asked to associate each word in this list with the type of person or animal with which it is commonly employed, that is, herd of cattle, swarm of bees, horde of barbarians, drove of cattle, crowd of people, pack of wolves, gang of thieves, flock of sheep, group of men, and clan of Scotsmen. Group is used of inanimate objects, as well as of human beings, but is not ordinarily used of animals.

5 An estuary is the broad mouth of a river in which the water is influenced by the tide. There are no tides in the Great Lakes, because the volume of water is too small to be perceptibly influenced by the attraction of the moon. Therefore, the rivers emptying into such bodies of water have no estuaries in the strict sense of the term. Sometimes the estuary is thought of as a long arm of the sea instead of as the mouth of the river. A fiord is an inlet of the sea, characteristic of Scandinavian countries. Large sand dunes are found at the southern end of Lake Michigan. Sand dunes travel by reason of the action of the wind which carries the sand up the windward side and deposits it to leeward. Dunes will destroy forests in their onward march. Some famous isthmuses of the world are Panama, Suez, Corinth.

6 No comment is required except to ask for description and function of the organs named in the list.

7 The fuselage of an airplane is the body or frame. Tonneau is the body of an automobile. Aileron is the movable part of the wing of an airplane. The chassis is the underframe of an automobile, including the wheels and driving mechanism.

8 It would be well to ask the pupils for the historical or geographical significance of some of these rivers. Call attention to the fact that for rivers of the Western Hemisphere, we put the proper name first, while for rivers of the other hemisphere, we generally put the word "river" first. For example, we speak of the Ohio River, but the River Rhine. The River Nile is famous for its periodic inundations with resultant deposits of fertile soil.

Exercise II-2

1 Pupils should be asked to suggest a corresponding male or female for the words in this list: cow, ram, bullock, hen, stag, duck, ewe, bull, cock, doe. The game of ducks and drakes

is played by skipping flat stones across the surface of the water.

2 A mesa is a plateau with steep sides. The word is Spanish for table. The word "gorge" means throat, and is applied to any narrow passage. It is also applied to a mass of material which obstructs a narrow passage, such as "ice gorge." To "gorge oneself" really means to eat until one is full up to the throat. A divide is the ridge of a mountain range from which streams flow in opposite directions.

3 Pupils should be asked to give the corresponding feminine names: Henrietta, Josephine, Louise, Georgiana.

4 Marble is a form of limestone which has been subjected to great heat and pressure in the bowels of the earth. Tufa, or tuff, is a porous rock of volcanic origin, usually stratified. The catacombs in the city of Rome were dug through tufa. In a strictly scientific sense, tufa is applied only to deposits from springs. Terra-cotta is an Italian word for baked clay. Stucco is plaster for coating walls. A fine plaster is used for inside walls and a coarse variety containing cement for outside walls.

5 Transmission is primarily an abstract noun, but since in the automobile it is the name of a definite part of the machine, it must be classed here as a concrete noun. The differential is a device which enables the rear wheels of the automobile to move at different rates while turning a corner. Each wheel delivers power at its own speed.

6 A mace was a heavy war club, often studded with spikes, used in the Middle Ages. The mace is also a staff carried before a dignitary as a sign of authority. A mortar may be described as a sawed-off cannon. It is used to throw heavy shells at low velocity. A mortar is also a heavy bowl which chemists use for pulverizing substances by means of a pestle. The weapon known as the torpedo is named after a fish which paralyzes its victim by an electric discharge. The catapult was an ancient military machine used for shooting arrows. It was similar to, but usually smaller than, the ballista, which was used for throwing stones. The battering ram was a heavy beam used for undermining or demolishing walls. It was so named because it had a metal head resembling the head of a ram. A pike was a long wooden shaft with a steel point used in the manner of a bayonet.

7 A vice is a habit of mind rather than an action, though it reveals itself in action. The five vices named here are found in the list of the seven capital sins, the other two being lust and gluttony. These vicious qualities are called sins because they dispose us to commit sinful acts. Arson is the malicious burning of another's house or other building, or the willful burning of one's own house for the purpose of collecting insurance. Larceny is the same as theft. Grand larceny differs from petit larceny in regard to the amount of the theft. The standard differs in different states. A felony is a serious criminal offense, that is, treason, murder, arson, robbery, and so forth. Perjury is the violation of an oath. It usually refers to the giving of false testimony in court after having sworn to tell the truth.

Exercise II-3

1 These animals may also be divided into domestic and wild, since in certain parts of the world the elephant is trained to do useful work. Herbivorous animals are usually nonaggressive, though they may be very formidable when interfered with.

2 Oboe is a corrupted form of hautboy which is a modification of the French "hautbois" which means "high wood"; that is, a wooden musical instrument of high pitch. The guitar is a long-necked instrument having six strings. The zither has thirty or forty strings. Both of these words come from the Greek word "cithara." The ukulele has four strings.

3 The word "sundry" means several or various.

5 The French noun melée comes from the verb meler, to mix.

6 Copse is short for coppice, a thicket of small trees. A moor is a tract of waste sandy ground overlaid with peat, often marshy. Steppe is the name given to prairies in Russia. A chaparral is a dense thicket of evergreen oaks found in Mexico and southwestern United States.

7 An adze is an axe with a thin, curved blade placed at right angles to the handle.

8 The primary meaning of epoch is an important event, though

it is usually used as a synonym for era; however, it is more specific than era. They both refer to a period of time characterized by a new order of things, changes of great importance, and so forth.

Exercise II-4

1 The crow and the raven belong to the same family. They have glossy black feathers. The adjective gullible does not come from gull as used in this list. It comes from the verb "to gull" meaning to deceive or cheat. This in turn comes from an obsolete noun "gull" which meant an unfledged bird, and was applied to an unsophisticated person.

2 Diagram related adverbs of place and of time as follows, and explain meaning.

Where	whence	whither	Now	henceforth	hitherto
Here	hence	hither	Then	thenceforth	thitherto
There	thence	thither			

3 Steed is the only word on the list which has an exclusively laudatory connotation. A mongrel is a dog of mixed and uncertain breed.

4 The earth is a spheroid. The centrifugal force produced by its rotation causes it to be slightly flattened out at the poles. Compare pyramid and cone. In the strict sense an oval is not the same as an ellipse. An oval is larger at one end than at the other, that is, it is egg shaped.

5 A yacht may be propelled by a sail or motor. A kayak is an Eskimo canoe covered with a deck which leaves only a small opening near the center to admit the occupant. The occupant wears a circular cloak or cape which is fastened to the edges of the canoe in such a way as to exclude water.

6 A hamper is a large basket usually provided with a cover. A carafe is a water bottle used at table. A demijohn is a large bottle usually enclosed in wickerwork.

Exercise III-1, A

Pupils should be asked to designate the specific relationship that exists between the first two members. This, of course, should correspond to the relationship that exists between the third and fourth. For example: "floor" is that part of a room on which we walk; the brush is the tool of the painter; pound is a unit of measurement; mortar is a binding element. The wheel and the runner serve the wagon and the sled respectively, firstly, as a means of support; secondly, as a means of counteracting friction. Pupils will say that the wheel makes the wagon move. This is true only of a power vehicle. The knife is the cutting tool for wood, while a bow is the instrument for producing music from a violin. Pupils may suggest that the finger is used sometimes in playing the ukulele. This would not be a good answer, for the finger is not a tool, but a part of the musician. In problem seven, various units of electricity may be used. The volt is the unit of pressure; the ampere, the unit of current; the watt, the unit of power, and so forth.

Exercise III-1, B

In the second section of this drill, pupils may have difficulty in filling in the second and third terms unless they devise some technique. For instance, they should try to combine the first and the fourth terms so as to make sense out of the combination. For example: a glove for the foot is an absurdity, but immediately suggests hand for glove and shoe for foot; incidentally, the German word for glove is "hand-shoe."

12 Horses are not kept in kennels. What are they kept in, and what is kept in a kennel?

13 Since the fourth term is an animal, the pupil should reason that the second term must be an animal. Now what animal do you associate with "cat"? Only three are familiar; dog, rat, or mouse. Dog evidently does not help us, but a rat or mouse is the traditional prey of the cat. If we ask what animal chases the rabbit, our problem is solved.

16 The lion is the king of animals; and the eagle is the king of birds. The lion is the traditional symbol of courage, but no animal has true courage. A dog may be trained by his master to show

something of courage, but this is quite different from rational courage as found in man.

18 The "out" of baseball, and the "down" of football have this in common: They put an end to a particular play and a certain definite number of each puts an end to the scoring opportunities of the side on the offensive.

19 Leaves of trees are analogous to lungs of animals in as much as they are organs for the exchange of gases. Only the under side of the leaf serves as a lung, for the top side is glazed as a protection against too rapid evaporation.

21 Cotton and wheat are the staple products of Alabama and Minnesota, respectively. Any "cotton" state may replace Alabama.

22 The word "quarry" has another meaning, that is, the prey of an animal or bird.

23 The wigwam and the igloo are the traditional dwellings of the Indian and the Eskimo, respectively, although neither of these dwellings are in use today.

Exercise III-2, A

1 The bark of the tree and the shell of the turtle are naturally produced surfaces for the protection of the organism.

4 The basic rhythm of poetry is relatively regular, while the rhythm of prose has no definite pattern.

5 Caterpillar comes from the French and means "fuzzy cat."

7 Electricity flows along the outside of the wire, rather than through it, although the current does involve a motion of the electrons in the wire. In the study of physics a great deal is made of the analogy between water and electricity.

8 The facial expressions associated with the emotions are natural reactions which do not have to be learned by imitation.

Exercise III-2, B

In the second part of the drill pupils may be asked to construct a metaphor based on each of these proportions, and to express this metaphor in a sentence. The difference between simile and metaphor may be discussed.

12 Both jealousy and worm are agents of destruction which bore from within. The egg from which the worm is hatched is deposited by the moth in the blossom before the fruit is formed.

15 Graft and parasites both derive unearned sustenance from their hosts. The parasitic vine draws sap from the tree to which it clings; the grafter makes illegal profit from the political position which he holds.

Exercise III-3

2 Pupils should be required to name or explain all relationships. Thus in this problem, food and drink are to be classified as the natural objects of their respective appetites.

3 The sole and the palm are the contact surfaces of the foot and hand respectively.

6 The leopard is also called the panther. The American leopard is the jaguar.

8 Hercules, famed for his strength, was a demigod. Mercury was an Olympian deity. The metal mercury, known also as quicksilver, that is, living silver, is named after him.

9 Perhaps some member of the group can explain the refining processes by which iron and gasoline are obtained.

10 The faucet and the switch are means of arresting or of releasing flow. A faucet is sometimes referred to as a spigot, though the latter is properly a peg used to close the opening of a cask.

11 Jazz and slang are perverted forms of music and of language respectively.

13 Here and now express nearness to the speaker in regard to place and time; there and then indicate remoteness. Note that these terms may be paired in two ways.

19 Name the playing areas for other sports, that is, court, links, rink, and so forth.

22 Name other meats and the animals from which they are derived, that is, pork, venison.

24 Wine and hard cider are products of natural fermentation. Brandy is produced from these and from other fermented fruit juices by distillation.

25 Have pupils name personal attributes or spheres of action of other fabled deities, for example, Neptune, god of the sea; Pluto, god of the nether world; Venus, goddess of beauty.

Exercise III-4

2 The crosier represents a shepherd's staff. It is symbolic of the bishop's office as the spiritual shepherd of his flock.

5 The minaret is a lofty tower attached to a mosque. It is surrounded by one or more balconies from which the official crier announces the hour of prayer.

6 A sextant is an instrument by which a mariner measures the angular distance of the sun above the horizon at a given hour in order to compute his latitude and longitude and thereby determine his position. A transit is a form of theodolite. The full name is transit theodolite.

9 Fleur-de-lis means "flower of the lily." A conventionalized form is used in decorations and in heraldry.

11 Alchemy was a pseudoscience. It was practiced by men who were looking for a panacea, that is, a cure for all ills, as well as for a formula for changing baser metals into gold. It was the forerunner of scientific chemistry. Astrology is referred to in exercise I-3.

12 The olive branch as a symbol of peace is based on the story

of the dove that came back to the Ark with an olive branch in its beak. This was interpreted by Noe to indicate that the flood waters were subsiding.

19 The cypress is an evergreen often found planted in cemeteries.

20 The hammer and sickle combination is the symbol of the Soviet Union.

21 The egg-and-arrow design is often found used as a decoration for altars. It is symbolic of sacrifice, that is, the arrow represents death, the egg represents life.

22 Alpha and Omega are the first and last letters respectively of the Greek alphabet. Hence they stand for the beginning and the end. The two letters are often found on altars, vestments, and other sacred objects as a symbol of God, who is the first beginning and last end of all creation. The words are found in Apocalypse I.8.

24 The ermine is a species of weasel whose coat turns pure white in winter, except for the black tip of the tail. A judge's robe is traditionally lined with ermine as an emblem of integrity.

25 As Milton is the greatest epic poet not in world literature but only in English, the corresponding dramatist should be Shakespeare, not Sophocles, and so forth.

Exercise IV-1

In this exercise pupils will manifest a great deal of confused thinking and will want to defend their personal opinions, at least to the extent of claiming that their answers are not entirely wrong. As a matter of fact, in this exercise a greater variety of correct answers are found than is the case in other exercises. When a pupil insists on defending an unreasonable answer he should be asked to imagine himself proposing his answer to a jury of fairly well-educated, professional men, and to ask himself what answer he would expect them to give. This device tends to introduce a certain amount of objectivity into the pupil's thinking.

1 The attraction of the moon causes the water to bulge up, as it were, not only in the direction of the moon, but also on the

opposite side of the earth, thus giving two tides each day. The tide on the opposite side of the earth is due to centrifugal force, but it is not advisable to discuss this point with ordinary pupils. The sun also attracts the ocean, but to a lesser extent than the moon. When it pulls with the moon we have an especially high tide, called a spring tide.

2 The Bronx is one of the five boroughs into which the city of New York is divided. The other four are: Manhattan, Queens, Brooklyn, and Richmond.

3 Tobacco, in one sense, is the cause of nicotine; the tobacco plant produces nicotine. But, generally speaking, we would look upon tobacco as the source of nicotine; that is, we go to the tobacco plant to get nicotine.

5 Immunity is always the purpose of vaccination, but it is not always the effect. Therefore "effect" is not a good answer.

6 Jealousy may be the cause of or the source of quarrels.

8 Taxes are a source of revenue. Other sources of public revenue are duties, imports, and income from government-owned property.

10 "Orient" comes from the Latin and means "rising," that is, rising sun. The Orient is the Far East. The Near East is the Levant which is the French word for "rising."

11 The following answers may be accepted: species, effect, part, or based on.

12 Ask pupils what function a spring serves in a watch. They will probably endeavor to answer without recalling that a watch has two springs; one for the storage of power, the other for the regulation of movement. Work up this proportion: Balance wheel is to watch, as pendulum is to clock.

14 Carbon is material of diamond. Carbon is changed into a diamond by tremendous heat and pressure in the bowels of the earth. Small diamonds have been produced artificially by imbedding the carbon in molten iron. Diamonds can be destroyed by fire. The diamond is the hardest substance and is used for cutting other

substances. Another form of carbon is graphite.

23 "Credit is based on honesty." The meaning of this expression is this: Because I know this man to be honest I will extend him credit. However, I am not forced to extend the credit. Therefore, honesty is not the cause of credit.

27 Tidal waves are caused by earthquakes in the ocean bed.

30 Pneumonia may be classed as either a species, or an effect of infection.

Exercise IV-2

2 Khedive was a title conferred by the Sultan of Turkey on his viceroy in Egypt. The title went out of use in 1914.

3 Air is called a conductor of sound, but carrier is the closest word in the list. Pathway is not a good choice, since pathway connotes a definite direction.

5 A horsepower is the power required to lift 33,000 pounds at the rate of one foot per minute. Very few horses have such strength.

6 Steam is invisible water vapor as found, for instance, in the inside of a boiler. When the vapor escapes and becomes white and visible it is mist rather than steam.

9 The orbit of the earth is not a true circle but an ellipse. Its average diameter is 186 million miles. Associate this with the speed of light, which is 186,000 miles per second. It would take light 1,000 seconds (or more than 16 minutes) to travel from one side of the earth's orbit to the other. How long does it take light to reach us from the Sun?

14 Wire is strictly a conductor of electricity.

15 Degrees of heat, in this and some other countries, are measured on the Fahrenheit scale. In science and in many European countries the Centigrade scale is used. The zero of this scale is at the temperature of freezing water, while the one hundred degree mark is at the boiling point of water.

16-17 The chairman in a meeting and the umpire in a game are not really rulers, although this is the closest term to be found in the list. The chairman and the umpire regulate not what is to be done but how it is to be done. In football the umpire supervises defensive plays, while the referee has charge of offensive plays and is the supreme arbiter of the game.

20 Books may be called the source, the outlet, or the carriers of information, according to one's point of view.

21 Blushing is a reddening of the face due to a feeling of shame or confusion. It is probably due to the fact that nature is making a frantic effort to send a large supply of blood to the brain to meet the emergency of finding a quick explanation for a compromising situation.

22 Typhoid fever should not be confused with typhus fever. The latter is a virulent plague which often breaks out in time of war or of some great disaster.

25 The channel of a river may be called the pathway of the current. It would scarcely be called an outlet or a carrier.

26 A chimney should be called an outlet for smoke, rather than a pathway, in view of the fact that the smoke is not headed for a definite goal.

Exercise IV-3

2 Notice that there is no "e" in lightning.

5 Discuss the difference between "transparent" and "translucent." A translucent object admits the passage of light, but does not permit clear vision. Frosted glass is translucent but not transparent.

10 A tabloid is a compressed portion of food or drugs. The word is popularly applied to a newspaper with a reduced size of page and condensed news items.

16 To create means to make out of nothing. To annihilate means to reduce back to nothingness. In a strict sense, only God can create or annihilate.

24 Hay fever is an allergic disease, that is, a disease caused by undue sensitivity to substances which are not injurious to the general population.

28 Ductility is the quality of a metal which permits it to be drawn out into wire. Malleability is the quality of a metal which permits it to be beaten into various shapes.

30 Meekness is not the same as faintheartedness. Meekness is the virtue through which a high-spirited person controls the passion of anger.

32 The plastic arts are sculpture and ceramics, that is, pottery. Plastic surgery is the art of repairing or replacing injured or missing parts of the body.

Exercise IV-4

In all cases where the relationship is one of analogy, it will be profitable to ask the pupils to formulate a proportion, that is, wing is to bird as fin is to fish.

5 Flow of electricity is measured in amperes; resistance is measured in ohms.

7 Anesthetic comes from the Greek word "aisthetikos" (able to feel) to which the negative prefix "an" has been added. Esthetic means gifted with refined powers of perception, especially in the field of art.

9 Digit is the common term that includes fingers and toes. It is used chiefly of animals.

12 Fish get their supply of oxygen from the air that is dissolved in water. A fish would smother to death if placed in water that had been previously boiled, since boiling drives off air.

15 Specific gravity is measured in relation to water. If a cubic inch of a given substance has the same weight as a cubic inch of water, the substance is said to have a specific gravity of one. Mercury has a specific gravity of 13, since it weighs thirteen times as much as an equal volume of water.

22 Streamlining increases speed of an airplane or a ship by eliminating the eddy currents of air or water respectively.

32 Sap does not circulate in plants. It rises from the roots and passes slowly through the trunk and branches into the leaves, where the watery content is gradually lost through evaporation. Carbon dioxide is taken in through the leaves, is dissolved in the sap, and makes its way through the sap to the branches and trunk.

Exercise VI-1

1 Pupils will often write "body of water" instead of "stream." "Body of water" would rather be applied to a pond, lake, or ocean. Ask pupils the meaning of rill, brook, rivulet.

2 Call attention to the importance of each qualifying word by asking what the chair would become if not movable, if lacking a back, if made for more than one person, and so forth.

3 What would the square become if only the opposite sides or the opposite angles were equal? Answer: a rectangle or a rhombus respectively. If only opposite sides <u>and</u> opposite angles were equal, we would have a rhomboid.

4 Call attention to the fact that the modern rifle was developed from the old musket of Civil War days by the insertion of spiral grooves (called rifling) on the inside surface of the barrel. These grooves impart to the bullet a rotary motion which prevents it from turning sideways in its flight, and thus secures greater accuracy. A carbine is shorter and lighter than a rifle and has no provision for a bayonet.

6 The buoyancy of a balloon is measured by the difference between the weight of the gas in its envelope and the weight of an equal volume of air which it displaces. Hydrogen was the gas originally used in balloons, but it has been superseded, especially in dirigibles, by helium which is noninflammable.

7 Pupils may write "propelled by pedals acting on a chain." This is not a good answer as the pedals transmit rather than produce power.

8 Pupils should be reminded that in a philosophical sense any sentient organism is an animal, such as, fish, birds, worms, insects, and so forth.

9 Elasticity is the power of a body to recover its original shape after being deformed (stretched, compressed or bent) by an outside force. Popularly, elasticity is measured by the amount of distortion from which a body will recover; but scientifically, it is measured by the power which the body exerts in returning to its original shape. Hence scientifically steel is many times more elastic than rubber.

Exercise VI-2

1 There are three situations in which it is lawful to take human life: in self-defense, in time of war, and, on the part of the state, in the enforcement of law. Yet even in these situations, certain conditions must be fulfilled before the act can be justified.

2 Rhythm is the regular recurrence of a phenomenon, that is, of any event that can be perceived by the senses. Examples of rhythm are: the return of day and night, or of the seasons of the year, the beating of the heart, breathing, and so forth.

3 Discuss the difference between envy and jealousy. In envy the success of another person makes us sad by reminding us of our inferior position, but his success does not of itself hinder us from enjoying similar success. Jealousy will arise only if the other person's success involves loss or disappointment to us, or puts us in his power. Envy is always bad, but jealousy may be a good quality, for example, when it leads us to defend our rights against unlawful intrusion. We may envy another's wealth, we may be jealous of a successful rival in politics, love, and so forth. We should be jealous of our liberty and of our good name.

5 Discuss the expressions: "on the block," "under the hammer," "knocked down to the highest bidder."

6 Science refers to systematized knowledge, art refers to the way of doing or making something.

7 An "overt" act is an outward act that can be witnessed by others. Compare the two words, "covert" and "overt."

8 Dueling is now discountenanced in most civilized countries. It is of course a serious violation of the natural law.

9 Biology (the science of life) is a broad term which covers many related but distinct fields. Its chief subdivisions are botany and zoology.

10 The four elements in worship are: adoration, thanksgiving, reparation, and impetration.

11 Compare metaphor with metonymy. Metaphor is based on resemblance, metonymy is based on any other relationship, such as those of cause and effect, container and contents, part and whole, nearness in time or space, and so forth.

12 There are three kinds of equilibrium: stable equilibrium, in which the displaced object tends to return to its original position; unstable equilibrium, in which the displaced object tends to depart still farther from its original position; and neutral equilibrium, in which a displaced object remains at rest in the new position, for example, a round object on a level plane surface.

Exercise VI-3

Before the pupils attempt to do this exercise, they should be given some brief practice in reducing figurative expressions to literal language. Some will not find this easy. We often use figurative language in everyday speech without being conscious of it, and some pupils will have a tendency to substitute a new figure for the one that they are interpreting instead of expressing the thought in strictly literal terms. Failure to grasp the distinction between figurative and literal expressions will make it difficult to succeed in this exercise.

The following expressions may be used for practice:

a "That argument was a home run" means "That argument was very effective."

b "Every cloud has a silver lining" means "Every misfortune is accompanied by some advantage." To say "Every misfortune has a bright side" would be to introduce a new metaphor, less vivid than the first but still a metaphor.

c "The news of his death came like a bolt from the blue" means "The news of his death came as a complete surprise." It was an unexpected as a thunderbolt from a clear sky.

3 This figure is taken from the Bible. In Matthew V 15, we read, "Neither do men light a candle and put it under a bushel, but upon a candle stick, that it may shine to all that are in the house." In this passage Christ is urging his disciples not to be ashamed of their good works but to perform them openly.

4 Any strong emotion has a tendency to interfere with clear thinking and good judgment and is therefore aptly compared with alcoholic intoxication which has the same general effects. The emotion aroused by success is self-esteem and self-love.

5 Jaundice is a diseased condition in which the skin assumes a yellow color due to the presence of bile in the blood. In extreme cases the bile invades the cornea of the eye and causes the patient to see everything as if tinted with yellow. A person with an envious or sour disposition sees nothing but evil in the lives and actions of others.

6 Some metals, especially silver, lose their luster on account of the action of certain chemicals in the air. Our reputation becomes "tarnished" if our actions give grounds for suspicion.

8 A debater's rebuttal will "miss the mark" if the debater fails to understand the point of his adversary's argument.

Exercise VI-4

1 Some primitive tribes were in the habit of dipping their arrows in poison so as to insure the death of their victims, even though the arrow did not reach a vital spot. Sarcasm should be distinguished from irony. Irony is a form of expression, either humorous or bitter, in which intended meaning is the opposite of the literal sense of the words. Sarcasm is always bitter and cutting. It is often, but not always, ironical.

3 A pall is a heavy cloth, usually of a dark color, used to cover a coffin.

4 "Zooming" is an imitative word suggestive of the sound made by the motor of an airplane when the aviator, after gliding downward with power cut off, suddenly throws on full power and begins a rapid ascent.

5 A rapier is a straight two-edged sword with narrow blade used for thrusting. A bludgeon is a short club with one end loaded or thicker than the other. To parry is to ward off a blow, especially in fencing, by the skillful use of one's own weapon.

7 A catacomb is an underground passage with recesses in the walls for the burial of the dead. The early Christians in Rome gathered in these vaults for the holding of religious services.

9 Carnival, which means "the taking away of meat," is the name given in Latin countries to a period of gaiety and feasting immediately preceding Lent. The Mardi Gras festival is an example of it. The term is now applied to any period of merrymaking.

10 Flotsam is the floating wreckage of a ship or its cargo. Jetsam is cargo thrown overboard to lighten a ship in a storm.

INSTRUCTIONS FOR TUTORS

When your pupils have assembled for the first meeting, call their attention to the fact that they have already received a two-page explanation of the nature and purpose of the course and that this will obviate the need of preliminary remarks on your part. However, if they have not received this explanatory material, it will be desirable to give them a brief summary of its contents.

Distribute the drill papers and instruct the students to read carefully the instructions given at the top of the page. There should be no preliminary discussion of the exercise, since one of the objectives of the course is the development of ability to comprehend and follow written instructions. Warn pupils against the inefficiency of either working too rapidly, or of delaying too long over any single problem. Announce that time will be called at the end of fifteen minutes, or when three fourths of the group have completed the work. During the writing period, observe attitudes manifested by individual pupils and make a note of your observations for future reference. It is not advisable to inspect the work of the pupils while they are writing, or to offer suggestions, as such action is more distracting than helpful. When three fourths of the group have finished, announce that one minute will be given for the others to record any answers that they may have ready.

At the end of the writing period, call upon one of the pupils to report on his answer to the first problem. If the answer is correct, ask if any one else has a different answer which he would like to propose. If two or three acceptable answers are given, invite the class to determine which of the answers is more significant, more scientific, more practical, and so forth. If the first answer is incorrect, call upon another member of the class to criticize it. The critic should not be allowed merely to give his own solution. He should be required to point out the defectiveness of the previous answer, and then propose his own solution. If no debate should develop in regard to the solution of the problem, open a discussion by asking some pertinent question on a topic suggested by the subject matter of the problem.

Make sure that the pupils understand not only the solution of the problem but also the meanings of all the words occurring in it. The acquisition of an adequate vocabulary is not the least of the objectives to be aimed at in the course. From time to time suggest how processes exemplified in the drills may be used in regular academic work or in business and professional life. Any comments that will throw light on the technique of correct thinking, or which will inspire interest in thinking as a liberal art, will be in keeping with the purposes of the course.

The computation of scores is intended to promote interest rather than to determine proficiency, yet it is possible that tabulated scores will be of some value in giving a profile of the mental equipment of the students. Let the pupils compute their own scores under your general supervision. In case of doubt, decide in favor of the pupil. At the end of the course, file the record of scores with the director. It is not desirable that copies of the drills should circulate among the other students in the school, since previous acquaintance with the problems would diminish interest if they should at a later date decide to enroll in the course. Hence do not issue more than one copy to each member of your group and collect all copies at the end of the class period.

PRACTICAL HINTS

1 Seat your pupils in a large semicircle. This will secure a "round-table" atmosphere and will remind the pupils that they constitute a discussion group rather than a formal class. In general, pupils should address their remarks to you rather than to one another. Insist on courtesy and the use of correct English.

2 As long as your group is able to maintain discussion, you should function as an impartial chairman, but when a difficult problem gets beyond their control, you should assume the role of instructor and make use of all of your pedagogical skill, including the use of the blackboard.

3 Do not permit lengthy discussions on the meanings of words. Have recourse at once to the dictionary. Let one of the pupils look up disputed meanings and pronunciations. Suggest that pupils keep a list of all new words met with in each class period.

4 Do not praise or criticize pupils directly. Rather remark on the excellence or defectiveness of their answers. Give credit for the good points contained in defective answers, and if possible, offer your solution as an improvement rather than a correction.

5 Accept appreciatively all factual data offered by the pupils, especially if a contribution seems to have been derived from personal experience or research. If insoluble problems arise,

promise to secure definite information for the next meeting, or better still, invite one of the pupils to volunteer to look up the matter in a reference book.

6 For the first two or three classes at least, do not indulge in humorous remarks, and in general, do not make reference to yourself or to your own personal experiences.

7 It is not necessary that all problems be made subject matter of discussion. While preparing for class, select for purposes of discussion problems which seem to you most promising or with which you are most competent to deal.

8 It is important that the class be provided with correct answers to all problems in each exercise. Hence, a few minutes before the end of the period, break off the discussion and announce valid answers for all problems which you will not have time to discuss in detail. Do not carry over an unfinished exercise to the next meeting. Begin each class with a fresh drill.

9 Classes should be dismissed promptly at the end of the assigned period.

10 After each class, make a memorandum of any favorable or unfavorable impression made on you by individual pupils. This will facilitate the task of checking the personality-rating chart at the end of the course.

REMEDIAL WORK

An important objective in the Course in Effective Thinking is the recognition and the correction of defective mental attitudes and of personality traits which interfere with correct thinking. The purpose of these instructions is to indicate some of the ways in which student tutors may help in the attainment of this objective. It is to be understood, of course, that not all defects are amenable to correction, and not all remediable defects can be treated successfully by novice teachers. In some pupils the root causes of certain faults are so difficult to discover that only a psychological expert can analyze the situation. In others, the undesirable habit, although easily understood, is so deeply implanted in the personality that not much can be done about it. On the other hand, many simple cases will be found which will respond to easily applied remedies. A number of such cases will be described here and it is hoped that even student tutors will be able to help their pupils to eliminate some of their faulty reactions. In most cases the remedial work should be done in private interviews, but often enough, desirable results may be achieved by means of general observations directed to the class as a whole rather than to any individual pupil. Much will depend upon the spirit of the group and upon the geniality of the tutor's personality.

Typical Defects and Methods of Treatment

Aloofness — Some pupils will manifest an unwillingness to take part in the discussions. They will never ask a question, propose an objection, or express an opinion, even when called upon. This attitude is usually due to timidity, even when there are appearances of sullenness. It frequently happens that such pupils finally succumb to the example of their classmates and become active participants in discussions. However, if no improvement is noted after six or seven lessons, the tutor should call the pupil for a brief conference and emphasize the fact that facility in self-expression is one of the major objectives of the course.

If the pupil explains his habitual silence on the score that he can never think of anything to say and that his ideas always seem foolish when he attempts to express them, the tutor should call attention to some of the really good answers which without doubt he will be able to find in the pupil's written work. Such answers prove that the pupil is inferior to his classmates only in self-assurance. He should then be persuaded to make at least one spontaneous contribution to the discussion each day. He will then learn by experience that in giving expression to some of the ideas which he has, he will stimulate his mind to think of a great many more.

Volubility — Other pupils, on the contrary, tend to obstruct the work of the class by monopolizing the discussion. As soon as the tutor recognizes this problem, he should summon the offender, and after congratulating him on his interest, call attention to the fact that his well-meant but excessive eloquence is somewhat unfair to the more timid members of the class. If this remonstrance goes unheeded, the director should be consulted. The director may find through a confidential interview that the pupil's volubility is due to an exaggerated desire for attention and publicity, or to a vivacious nature which on account of certain enviromental restraints finds no other outlet for its energy.

Timidity of Manner — Pupils will sometimes give their answers in a timid, indistinct voice which indicates lack of self-confidence and a fear of making an unfavorable impression. The tutor should explain that a fearless exposition of one's ideas is a sign of one's trust in the fairmindedness and good will of others. It is therefore a mark of a wholesome personality and paves the way for true popularity. Tell the diffident pupil: By showing timidity in self-expression, you are not paying a great compliment to the other members of the group. You are implicitly telling them: "I'm afraid of you folks. I don't trust you. If I let you see how I think or even how my voice sounds, you might be so impolite as to laugh at me."

Belligerency — When a pupil voices his opinions in a bold, challenging, or even belligerent tone, the tutor should be prepared to deal with a case of inferiority complex. Such a pupil may be over-compensating for a secret sense of intellectual inadequacy, or on the other hand, he may be releasing pent-up emotions which have had their origin in some other situation, for example, in a conflict with school authorities, or in unsatisfactory home conditions. In the latter case the tutor will probably be unable to be of much help, even if he recognizes the nature of the problem. However if the tutor suspects that the pupil is trying unconsciously to cover up intellectual timidity, he should offer the following advice: "You ought to have more confidence in the value of your ideas. Your reasoning is generally quite sensible and sound. Now good ideas do not need fireworks. They shine by their own light. A calm, deliberate tone is a sign of a deep thinker and makes a good impression, but people become suspicious and resentful when they find that someone is trying to force his ideas upon them."

Eccentricity of Viewpoint Occasionally pupils will try to defend an inept or bizarre answer, even after a sound answer has been accepted by the class. If this should prove to be a habitual reaction on the part of a given pupil, the tutor may have good reason to suspect that a secret desire of self-assertion rather than a love of objective truth is interfering with that pupil's reasoning processes by warping his judgment. Such a pupil should be told that while occasionally an individual may be in the right and a whole group may be in the wrong, the burden of proof is always on the individual, and therefore he should not insist on his views until after much thought he becomes convinced that the opposite position is untenable. A pupil who is habitually out of step with others should endeavor to find the reason for his perpetual difference of viewpoint. If he is successful in his quest, he will have made a great step forward in improving his mental efficiency as well as his social attractiveness.

Preoccupation with Exceptions A problem that often arises in this type of discussion is found in the attitude of some pupils who are always on the alert to attack a sound and generally accepted rule on the score that it is not absolutely universal in its application. The exceptional cases which they allege, may be real enough in themselves, but often they are not of sufficient consequence to warrant the rejection of the law which they seem to violate. Thus, the class may be quite ready to accept the statement that wood floats in water while stones do not. Yet some pupil may unduly stress the fact that certain species of wood in the unseasoned state will sink in water, and that pumice stone will actually float. If these facts are proposed as interesting bits of information, the contribution should be most welcome; but if the exceptions are urged against the validity of the general proposition, the discussion is brought to a standstill and the tutor has a problem on his hands.

If the tutor suspects that the objection is offered merely for the sake of showing off superior knowledge, he should recognize the value of the contribution, and then observe that mature minds do not reject general rules that happen to admit of rare and inconsequential exceptions. Scientific accuracy is a good thing, but good judgment and a sense of relative values are still more important. If this indirect approach does not prove effective, the tutor should consult the director as to the best method of suggesting to the obstructionist that his tactics are not conducive to popularity.

Often enough, however, the objector will be quite sincere. Some narrow and timid minds are quite paralyzed by the presence of an exception and are unable to assent to, much less make use of, generalizations which are not universally valid. Such pupils should be warned that this attitude will make it impossible for them ever to do any constructive thinking and that it will unfit them for coping with the practical problems of life. Even in the physical sciences, we meet with exceptions to general laws, and in such branches of knowledge as medicine, psychology, law, and business, progress can be made only by accepting generalizations that are not strictly universal in their application.

Vague Answers Sometimes the tutor will meet with pupils who are unwilling to give decisive answers to problems. They will endeavor so to qualify every statement that they cannot be convicted of error no matter what the true answer may turn out to be. They will tell you that pearls are sometimes found in oysters; that the moon has something to do with the tide; and that it would not be good for society if divorce became very common. These pupils should be told that such indulgence in vague answers will eventually react upon their mental acumen, and that it will prevent them from ever becoming clear thinkers. They should endeavor to make the above statements more precise. If they are not sure of their ground, they should indicate their uncertainty, not by blurring the concept itself, but by proposing it in the form of a clear-cut opinion. They should say, for instance: "I <u>think</u> that <u>pearls are produced by oysters</u>; I <u>think</u> that the moon is the <u>cause</u> of tides; I <u>think</u> that divorce is <u>contrary to the natural law</u>." Such statements have the merit of clearness, if not that of certainty, and they provide a satisfactory point of departure for an intelligent discussion.

Lack of Neatness Papers turned in by the pupils at the end of each class period should be inspected for spelling mistakes and for conspicuous lack of order and neatness. Attention should be called to these defects in private conference. If any apology is felt to be needed for such remedial measures, the tutor may begin by saying, "Do you mind if I make a suggestion? I have been asked by the director of the course to call attention to such defects as these. Such faults will count against you in the business and professional world, as well as in school work, and I am sure that you prefer to have them pointed out and corrected now, rather than to be handicapped by them later."

Some pupils habitually turn in papers on which answers have been changed not once but many times. This should be interpreted as a sigh of impulsiveness and lack of decision. These pupils should be told to think out their answers in advance, and not commit anything to paper until they are reasonably sure of what they want to say. The first answer should be allowed to stand until the pupil is convinced that a change will represent an improvement. Corrections should be made neatly. The incorrect word should not be "blacked out" so that it cannot be read. Such a habit is a sign of too great an emotional reaction to one's mistakes. A well-poised personality does not try to obliterate all traces of its mistakes. It is much more interested in making positive progress than in trying to forget that it ever was in error.

EMOTIONAL OBSTACLES TO CLEAR THINKING

1 When people have no confidence in their native ability, they pay little attention to the first answer that comes to them. They take for granted that it must be wrong, for how could they ever hit upon the right answer at the first attempt? Thus they do not give first answers any chance to prove their worth. This is a great mistake. First answers, if not entirely correct, are frequently very close to the truth. If you habitually turn your back upon them, you will, more often than not, be setting out in the wrong direction. You will be looking all over the house for the key that is in your pocket. Moreover, even if the first suggestion is not correct, it will give you a good starting point for a reasoning process. Find out why it will not work, and then you will have a good clue for discovering an answer that will work.

2 Other people hold on to a first answer too long. They are afraid that if it ever gets away, they will never find another. They try to argue that it must be right. They do not give themselves a chance to see that it may be wrong. They are like a man who forces a wrong key into the lock with a hammer, instead of making sure that there are no other keys to be had. Such students should trust their natural ingenuity to furnish them with plenty of new suggestions if they will only release their panicky grip on the first.

3 Stubbornness in holding on to a first opinion is often enough due to pride. To give up one's first answer is to admit that one was temporarily in error. Some people do not like to admit, even to themselves, that a wrong idea could ever enter their heads. That would spoil their record. Hence they try to make believe that if their first answer were understood in the right way, it would be a good answer. Such intellectual insincerity is a sign of an inferior personality, if not of an inferior mind. A truly great mind is quick to recognize its own mistakes, and glad to correct them.

4 An improper attitude toward obvious answers is a frequent source of inefficiency. Timid minds are prone to suspect that obvious, common-sense answers are too simple to be correct, and they never give such answers a wholehearted welcome. Proud minds, on the other hand, are not willing to be satisfied with an answer that anybody could give. That would be unworthy of their superior intelligence, and so they waste time in looking for lofty solutions which usually prove to be absurd.

5 Some people are poor listeners. They feel that it is humiliating to follow the lead of another mind during the course of an explanation. They are not really looking for the truth, but for an opportunity to show that they are in possession of the truth already. They are forever questioning and objecting, or else they make frequent comments, which are calculated to show that they are able to run ahead of the mind that is doing the explaining. They do not lend themselves to the author of a book, the professor in class, or even to their friends in conversation. Such people are not only inefficient; they are usually very unpopular.

6 Pupils who find difficulty in concentrating on their problems should not conclude that their minds are weak. They are usually mere victims of discouragement and fear of failure. Fear always makes us feel weak--makes us want to run away. The minds of these pupils are forever running away to some more pleasant topic, one that will not make them feel so inferior, for instance, prowess on the athletic field, or some social triumph. We are seldom bothered with distractions in matters where we have a sense of power.

There are, of course, other defects in thinking, such as indulging in vague answers in a subconscious effort to straddle a problem and be at least partly right; the habit of depending too much on others; the habit of quarreling with the wording of a question, and so forth. All of these false attitudes can be reduced to the basic faults of pride or fear, and all will be automatically cured by removing the underlying cause. Our final conclusion then should be: We can trust our minds to do the right thing if we only control the feelings of pride and fear.

Dear Student,

Now that you have enrolled in the Course in Effective Thinking, it is very important that you should know just what the course is expected to do for you. Your interest in the work and the profit that you will derive from it will both depend in large measure on your understanding of our objectives and our technique.

First of all, the drills used in the course are intended to teach you how to think. The process of thinking is not really a very mysterious affair. It consists basically in two simple operations: Comparison and Invention.

Comparison — Comparison consists in seeking differences and similarities between two objects, two people, two ideas, two situations, and so forth. For instance, if you were asked to write an essay on "Washington and Lincoln," a large part of your essay would consist in finding differences and similarities between these two men in regard to such things as their parentage, their early training, their physical appearance, their mental powers, their characters, and the historical periods in which they lived. The keener your mind is, the deeper and more subtle will be the differences and the similarities that you will notice in reading their biographies.

If you were asked to write an essay on airplanes, you would enumerate the various types of planes, and then proceed to show in what respects they are similar and in what respects they differ. Here again a keen mind would be able to find similarities and differences that would escape a less efficient mind.

Invention — The second type of thinking is called Invention. It is a process by which the mind endeavors to find or construct something that is needed for a special purpose. Invention requires a great deal of imagination. The following problems will illustrate what we mean by invention:

Find a word that will rhyme with opinion; make a list of all the things that you must bring with you on a fishing trip; find an argument that will induce your father to buy you a new car; devise a method by which a model airplane can be made to return to its starting point.

In the process of invention, the first step is to analyze the thing or the situation that you are going to improve or remedy. Make a list of all the qualities that the new element must possess; imagine what it will look like when you find it, and then go out and attempt to discover or manufacture it. For instance in the fishing problem mentioned above, you must first decide what kind of fish you wish to catch, where they are to be found, how long you will be away from home, who will go with you, and so forth. When these matters have been decided upon, you will be in a position to determine what you will need in the way of bait, equipment, food, clothing, means of conveyance, and the like.

Classification Classification is a further extension of analysis. It consists in an orderly arrangement in which similar things are put together and dissimilar things are kept apart. Doctors must be able to classify diseases; lawyers must classify cases; men in executive positions must be able to classify people, problems, processes, and expenses. Both in school work and in professional life, it is very important for you to possess skill in classification. This skill comes only with practice. You will get plenty of such practice in the Course in Effective Thinking.

Deep vs. Shallow Thinking One of the most important things to keep in mind when we are in search of differences and similarities is the contrast between deep thinking and shallow thinking. If I were to say that a whale resembles an elephant because both are large animals, I would be guilty of shallow thinking. The real resemblance is based on the fact that both are mammals and breathe with the aid of lungs. Steel differs from iron not merely because steel is hard and iron is soft, but chiefly because steel is an alloy and iron is a simple metal.

Remember this important rule of thinking: Shallow thinking consists in being satisfied with resemblances and differences based on outward appearances such as: size, shape, color, location, texture, price, and so forth.

Deep thinking, on the other hand, always looks first for differences and similarities that lie in the inner nature of things, such as: purpose, essence, function, origin, material, value, and so forth.

Some Samples of the Drills In order to train you in the use of these various mental operations, we have built up a set of drills which are very much on the order of puzzles. If you are to solve these puzzles successfully, you must become as versatile and agile in the mental field as a wrestler, a goalie, and an acrobat are in the realm of sport. When you get through with the drills used in this course, your ordinary school subjects ought to look quite simple and easy. Here are some samples:

In the following problems, you are asked to determine which term in each set of five does not fit in with the others. This term should then be replaced with one that is more appropriate. The first step is Comparison; the second is Invention.

Sedan, Zephyr, Cabriolet, Limousine, Roadster

Cotton, Wool, Silk, Alpaca, Mohair

Gulf, Isthmus, Strait, Bay, Estuary

In another type of drill you are required to practice comparison and invention in regard to relationships. Supply the missing terms in the following proportions:

General is to X as Y is to navy.

X is to morning as taps is to Y.

Telescope is to X as Y is to biology.

English Vocabulary A certain research agency has discovered that success in business and in professional life, as well as in school, depends upon the size of a man's vocabulary more than upon any other single factor. The *Course in Effective Thinking* will help you to expand your vocabulary, since in every drill you will meet with new words whose meanings will become clear to you during the discussion that follows each test. Keep a list of all the new words that you will meet with in each drill, study these lists from time to time, and make use of these words as soon as possible in your written and oral school work, and even in your daily conversation. Follow the same plan in regard to the new words that you will meet in your regular textbooks. If you want to know how much of a student you are, ask yourself how often you make use of the dictionary.

Self-Expression Remember that in the *Course in Effective Thinking*, each class group is an informal debating society. Make good use of the opportunity that the course gives you to practice self-expression. Two thirds of each class period is taken up with discussion. The more spirited the discussion, the more successful the class will be. Learn how to criticize defective answers given by other members of your group, but always express your opinion in good English and in courteous terms. Be ready to defend your own views when you are quite sure that they are well founded, but remember that the surest sign of intelligence is the ability to recognize one's own mistakes, either before or after the mistakes have been pointed out by others.

Course in Effective Thinking

Pupil.......................... Tutor ....

Course began............ Number of lessons taken....... Date.....

Report on Pupil's Work

Comes late	Often absent	Punctual
Slovenly posture	Slovenly work	Neat and orderly
Apathetic	Interest wanes	Sustained interest
Too deliberate	Overanxious	Expeditious
Helpless attitude	Ideas obstructed	Resourceful
Impetuous	Scatterbrained	Well poised
Inattentive	Ignores directions	Attentive
Lacks talent	Poor imagination	Talented
Poor home training	Poor school training	Well trained
Has read little	Not well informed	Wealth of ideas
Not observant	No curiosity	Very alert
Poor vocabulary	Poor self-expression	Expresses self well
Mentally stubborn	Likes to quibble	Docile
Makes excuses	Quarrels with task	Frank and honest
Misses the point	Reasons illogically	Thinks clearly
Timid in speech	Overbold	Well adjusted
Mentally immature	Emotionally immature	Mature for age
Mispronounces	Misspells	Accurate in P and S
Speech defect	Foreign accent	Speaks well
Poor eyes	Poor hearing	No defects
Nervous	Poor health	Good health

N.B. Single, double, or triple check indicates degree in which quality is present.